HARVESTERS

HARVESTERS

by
Irene M. Franck
and
David M. Brownstone

A Volume in the Work Throughout History Series

A Hudson Group Book

Facts On File Publications
New York, New York • Oxford, England

HARVESTERS

Library of Congress Cataloging-in-Publication Data

Franck, Irene M.
  Harvesters.

  (Work throughout history)
  "Hudson Group book."
  Bibliography: p.
  Includes index.
  Summary: Outlines the history of occupations
surrounding the collection and cultivation of food—from beekeeping, gardening, hunting, whaling, and fishing to farming of all kinds.
  1. Farmers—History. 2. Hunters--History. 3. Fishers
—History. 4. Agriculture—History. 5. Occupations—
History. [1. Agriculture—History 2. Occupations—
History] I. Brownstone, David M. II. Title.
III. Series.
S419.F73 1987   630'.9   86-24352
ISBN 0-8160-1444-2

10 9 8 7 6 5 4 3 2 1

Contents

Preface

Harvesters is a book in the multivolume series, *Work Throughout History*. Work shapes the lives of all human beings; yet surprisingly little has been written about the history of the many fascinating and diverse types of occupations men and women pursue. The books in the *Work Throughout History* series explore humanity's most interesting, important, and influential occupations. They explain how and why these occupations came into being in the major cultures of the world, how they evolved over the centuries, especially with changing technology, and how society's view of each occupation has changed. Throughout we focus on what it was like to do a particular kind of work—for example, to be a farmer, glassblower, midwife, banker, building contractor, actor, astrologer, or weaver—in centuries past and right up to today.

Because many occupations have been closely related to one another, we have included at the end of each article references to other overlapping occupations. In preparing this series, we have drawn on a wide range of general works on social, economic, and occupational history, including many on everyday life throughout history. We consulted far too many wide-ranging works to list them all here; but at the end of each volume is a list of suggestions for further reading, should readers want to learn more about any of the occupations included in the volume.

Many researchers and writers worked on the preparation of this series. For *Harvesters*, the primary researcher-writer was Douglass L. Brownstone; David G. Merrill and Thomas A. Crippen also worked on parts of this volume. Our thanks go to them for their fine work; to our expert typists, Shirley Fenn, Nancy Fishelberg, and Mary Racette; to our most helpful editors at Facts On File, first Kate Kelly and then James Warren, and their assistant Claire Johnston; to our excellent developmental editor, Vicki Tyler; and to our publisher, Edward Knappman, who first suggested the *Work Throughout History* series and has given us gracious support during the long years of its preparation.

Irene M. Franck
David M. Brownstone

Introduction

Harvesters are found in every culture in the world, for food is essential to all. Tens of thousands of years ago, while humans were still finding shelter in natural places like caves, they were "harvesting" the plant and animal life around them for food and other essential items such as clothing. So the harvesting occupations have a good claim to be considered the oldest occupations of all.

In that distant period, it was the *hunters* and *gatherers* who provided the food. The earliest hunters developed the basic techniques of tracking and trapping that continue to be used by their counterparts today. The main technical advances have come in the area of weapons used to kill the birds and animals that were their prey. For much of human history and in most cultures, hunting was a vital occupation, since it provided the meat necessary for survival. But in more modern eras, especially in countries with well-developed farms and ranches, those with money could buy meat without having to hunt for it. Among those parts of the population, hunting then was transformed into something of a sport.

Early humans also drew much of their food from plants. For many thousands of years they simply gathered the fruits, nuts, and seeds that grew around them. Then at some point, perhaps as early as 10,000 years B.C., they began to experiment with the planned and supervised growing of the plants that yielded them the most desired food. In the same period, they began to domesticate animals, nurturing them for food and other uses, and over the years learning how to breed the best animals for their purposes. So *farmers* and *ranchers* came into being. Especially in modern times, these have often specialized in growing certain types of plants or breeding certain kinds of animals—so now we have dairy farmers, orchardists, sheep ranchers, wheat farmers, and the like.

A few over the centuries have become so specialized that they have been considered separate occupations. *Beekeepers*, for example, have always been a breed apart, protecting their hives for the honey they produce—and at the same time providing a vital service to farmers, since the bees pollinate the plants and allow them to reproduce. *Gardeners* and *landscape designers* specialize in growing plants for more personal purposes, sometimes for private or medicinal use, but often for their sheer beauty.

Hunters had their counterparts on the waterways of the world: *fishers*. As hunters from the very earliest times in human history brought meat to the table, so those who lived on the shores of oceans, seas, rivers, and streams caught fish for food. While the seas have been most bountiful, the fisher's life has often been a hard one, filled with danger, especially out on the open water.

The waterways have seen specialists, too. For thousands of years, *divers* have been jackknifing under the water to bring up desirable seafood or precious items such as pearls and coral. To the dangers of the fishing life is added the danger of being cut off from a supply of air while underwater. Seafaring specialists of a different sort are *whalers*. These are fishers of the largest creatures that inhabit the seas, and their work has caused them to roam the world's oceans in search of their prey.

Whatever their specific tasks, harvesters provide most of the food and many of the by-products—from leather to perfume—desired by the peoples of the world. They are among the oldest and most important of the world's occupations.

HARVESTERS

Beekeepers

Before the development of complicated trading patterns that permitted the importing of sugar from tropical regions to cooler places, the principal natural sweetener available to humans was honey. It seems safe to assume that the plundering of wild beehives for their golden treasure was an important human activity in prehistoric times, spreading from the honey bee's original home in Asia. Before long, *beekeepers*—also called *apiarists*—had transformed honey from an occasionally found bonanza into a prized commodity and a lucrative business.

Beekeeping first became an active occupation in Egypt well over 2,000 years B.C. Each beekeeper built hives of thatch and mud and carefully placed them in locations where there were abundant fields of flowers to provide

1

pollen for the bees' honey production. Filling the waiting hives with industrious insects was the constant objective of the beekeeper. Some hives attracted bees because of their good locations, but the successful apiarist was constantly on the lookout for a wild swarm of bees to capture and install in a hive. The cry that a swarm had been sighted triggered instant reaction.

A swarm was an entire colony of bees—including a queen—migrating to a new location. It formed a dense cluster of interlocking bodies that would completely cover a tree limb or other surface as it paused on the way to its final destination. These swarms showed little of the active, stinging response that is the bee's trademark. The beekeeper was usually able to coax the swarm onto a convenient branch or piece of wood and carry the bees back to prepared hives without fear of being stung.

Once a colony had been installed in the artificially constructed hive, the beekeeper waited patiently as the bees worked. The mounting weight of the structure indicated the successful manufacture of honey by its inhabitants. All too often, the beekeeper's efforts were in vain. *Apiculture* (beekeeping), like agriculture and animal husbandry, was a risky business. Bad weather or disease could easily doom the honey harvest.

Removing the honey from the hive was an exceptionally messy and laborious job that changed little from the days of ancient Egypt until the mid-19th century, when technical advances were finally introduced. First, beekeepers had to quiet the bees by enveloping the hive with clouds of smoke, a practice still used today. The honeycombs then had to be cut from the hives by hand, pressed, and then strained to remove the honey. The remaining beeswax was also carefully preserved as a valuable item in itself.

Most of the bees died during this process, but many of them were able to sting the beekeeper first. Some beekeepers wore protective clothing such as long-sleeved shirts, pants or enveloping skirts, gloves, and gauze veils. But many professional beekeepers scorned any such protection and accepted stings as a minor inconvenience.

In ancient Egypt, beekeeping developed into a traveling profession. Hives of bees were placed on rafts on the Nile at the end of each October and poled slowly downstream to Cairo. Each stop along the way was timed to coincide with the flowering of a different crop in the four-month trip. It brought benefits to both the beekeepers and the *farmers* whose crops were pollinated by the journeying bees. The movement of hives of bees from field to field as an aid to both agriculture and honey production was practiced in most other civilized nations and continues to be an important component of successful fruit production in the United States and other countries.

Beekeeping was widely practiced in Mesopotamia by 500 B.C. and was well established in Greece by the fourth century B.C. A substantial body of literature about the practice of beekeeping dates from Greco-Roman times, notably the writings of Aristotle, Virgil, Pliny, and Cicero. Most Greek and Roman beekeepers were farmers who kept bees for extra income, though many well-to-do Roman farmers kept a specialist called a *mellarius*, who was in charge of overseeing and managing the bees.

Beekeepers have always had a somewhat dangerous but lucrative business, tending their hives. (From Diderot's Encyclopedia, *late 18th century)*

By 1000 A.D. there was a substantial trade in honey and beeswax both in England and without, following the long-standing pattern of export to Europe. During the late Middle Ages many English *bee masters* and *bee mistresses* gathered honey that was destined almost exclusively for shipment across the English Channel. Specialists provided the beeswax, for which there was also an active trade. It was sold in the markets to *chandlers* (candle-makers).

Wild hives were also owned, the many beekeepers establishing their claims by cutting an identifying mark on the tree trunk. Trees that might attract a wild swarm because of hollow trunks and nearness to flowering fields were jealously guarded and preserved by the beekeeper. *Bee walks*—paths that included valuable colonies of insects—were handed down from one generation to the next in wills.

Hives of honeybees were included among the baggage of the earliest European settlers in North America and escaping swarms quickly established themselves in the New World. Known as "white man's flies" by the Native Americans, bees became a common resource that enabled many settlers to earn additional incomes and set the basis for a major future industry.

Modern beekeeping developed in the middle of the 19th century. For the first time, innovations in hive design were introduced that allowed easy and profitable honey collection without the destruction of the colony. Removable honeycombs and centrifugal honey extractors transformed the industry, which until this new technology came along had seen no notable change from its simplest beginnings. With these innovations, beekeeping throughout the technologically influenced world became a widely followed, distinctly specialized full-time occupation. Associations and journals for beekeepers were started and the industry developed quickly, particularly in the United States. By the early 20th century, a single major honey producer in California could boast of a harvest of more than 125,000 pounds of honey (a single healthy hive may contain 60 pounds or more of honey) and employed a sizable work force to tend the 1,000 colonies of bees in his operation. Throughout the rest of the century, apiarists often followed the large-scale production pattern, hiring trained specialists to oversee honey production.

More than in many other forms of agriculture and animal husbandry, however, the smaller local producer has retained an important position in the marketplace. Still capturing swarms, using smoke to quiet the bees, and enduring bee stings, the beekeeper practices an occupation that bears striking resemblances to its earliest forms; for while the supporting technology has changed, the way bees manufacture honey has not.

For related occupations in this volume, *Harvesters*, see the following:

Farmers

Divers

There are basically two classifications of *divers*: skin divers, who make shallow dives for as long as they can hold their breath, and deep-sea divers, who, aided by breathing devices, are able to probe deeper waters for much more extended periods of time. Skin divers in ancient times were essentially *fishers*. As early as 4500 B.C., they dove into clear waters—notably the Mediterranean, where this activity flourished—in search of fish and other foodstuffs to feed their families. Nearly as early, divers were also used by armies to help provide them with food while on long and distant campaigns. Divers have continued to work as fishers in some parts of the world into modern times.

In later times, divers more often focused on bringing up desirable objects from the sea. One of the most precious items that skin divers became acquainted with was the pearl of the oyster. This is a rare stone because only a few oysters make pearls, and even fewer make them of gemlike quality. The Greeks and Romans dove for pearls, shells, and sponges, but Asia became the early center of this economic activity. Even before the Christian era, there were many commercial pearl fisheries, such as those in Ceylon (modern Sri Lanka). Ceylon fisheries were actively worked during the first thousand years B.C. and were famed for their production. Government control over the lucrative pearl fisheries was strict; the Ceylon fisheries' guard boats and lights were used to ensure that only government-authorized divers could fish for pearls. A manager called an *Adapanaar* directed the activities of the Indian *divers* who worked the pearl fisheries. That system would last with little change through the middle of the 19th century. Even so, some enterprising *poachers* always managed to snatch a portion of the wealth.

Pearl boats generally carried 13 crewmen and 10 divers. Each diver was paid one-quarter of what he collected. The pearl fishers' equipment was simple and their activity unchanged throughout the centuries. A 30-pound diving stone was tied to a long rope that could reach the sea bottom. Close to the stone a loop was knotted for the diver's foot and a large woven net rope was used to hold the pearl oysters. On command, the divers would plunge to the ocean floor in shifts of five and swiftly work in the shadowy depths to fill their containers. The best divers could remain underwater for 80 seconds and work at a depth of 80 feet, but most were limited to one minute at 55 feet. On reaching the limit of endurance, the diver yanked on his rope and was pulled to the surface.

The pearl fisheries were not without danger. A diver who became trapped between two rocks or misjudged his endurance after a grueling series of dives had little margin for error. Sharks prowling the warm waters of the pearl fisheries were always a menace, and before div-

Divers connected by rope or chain with a boat above have long brought up from the sea floor baskets of precious items such as pearls or sponges. (From Ocean World)

ing every diver was sure to ask a professional *shark-charmer* to recite some magic words that were supposed to protect the diver from danger.

Divers relying on rocks and lines went overboard wherever there were warm waters and suitable harvests of marine wealth. Pearl fisheries became established in many places, including the Persian Gulf (especially off the island of Bahrein), South America, the West Indies, and Australia, among other locations. In the Mediterranean, Greek and Turkish divers tore sponges from their underwater perches and clasped them under their arms as they returned to the waiting surface boats.

In modern times suits like this one have allowed divers to go ever deeper underwater, for scientific as well as commercial reasons. (Authors' archives)

Breathing appliances made deep-sea diving possible even in ancient times. Crude devices were developed for breathing underwater by the first century B.C., the most successful one being the hollow reed snorkel. Greater advances were made in modern times when divers became especially important to the navy. They were used to repair ships, recover lost or sunken items, and sometimes even to secretly inspect enemy positions. By 1300 A.D., a clear tortoise-shell goggle had been devised by the Persians for pearling. Military modification of the goggle soon followed, but it was not until after World War I that there was wide usage of the rubber-and-glass version.

The modern British navy made extensive use of divers and worked to modernize their equipment. In 1715 the British diver John Lathbridge developed a wooden-and-leather suit to be used by *salvage divers* (those who recovered sunken cargo). About a hundred years later, Augustus Siebe—a German who had made his home in England—devised the first truly modern deep-sea diving equipment. The development of independent breathing devices culminated in the *aqualung*, which made its appearance during World War II. In addition to this basic equipment, many diving vehicles have been invented to aid divers in their work.

Divers today do essentially the same jobs that they have done throughout history—repair, salvage, and fish. Even in the large commercial pearl fisheries in modern-day Japan, divers are needed to inspect breeding conditions and clean cages, for example. Some jobs for modern divers demand more than just diving skill. *Scientists* sometimes use divers to make studies of underwater life and geological conditions. Very often, though, scientists themselves do the diving, so that they can make their own observations. *Photographers* are used to film underwater scenes for scientific, military, and commercial purposes. Drilling companies employ divers to help them in their efforts to locate and extract offshore oil, natural gas, and manganese deposits.

Divers have always suffered occupational hazards from the excessive pressures exerted on their lungs. In the Middle Ages *breath-hold divers* were avid body (especially chest) builders. They compensated for their lack of protective equipment by improving their natural lung capacity and muscular support systems. Modern equipment, rather than alleviating divers' diseases and maladies, has actually added to them, by making possible frequent and excessively deep dives that were at one time deemed impossible. Osteonecrosis, an irreversible bone disease, is a common plague suffered by deep-sea divers. In this disease, fluctuating levels of blood supplied to the bone cortex cause the bone to actually wear away. The risk of getting this disease increases proportionately with the depth and length of the dive. Another serious problem is the "bends," the diver's name for decompression sickness. As a diver comes up from underwater, a too-rapid change in pressure causes nitrogen to collect in the body's joints and tissues. This can cut off oxygen, causing nausea, pain, shock, and even death. In modern times, deep-sea divers often enter decompression chambers to gradually adjust to the normal atmospheric pressure.

Increasingly, divers are asked to go deeper underwater and stay there longer, to satisfy the demands of mining, engineering, and offshore-drilling operations. This trend increases the likelihood of the diver's developing both osteonecrosis and diver's bends. Furthermore, in cold waters, divers are known to suffer from excessive body cool-downs that are occasionally fatal. This condition, known as hypothermia, is but one of the factors that has contributed to a high death rate among divers working on gas and oil installations in the North Sea.

For related occupations in this volume, *Harvesters*, see the following:

Fishers

For related occupations in other volumes of the series, see the following:

in *Artists and Artisans*:
Photographers

in *Manufacturers and Miners*:
Miners and Quarriers
Well-Diggers and Drillers

in *Scientists and Technologists*:
Biologists
Geologists

in *Warriors and Adventurers*:
Sailors

Farmers

The point at which people began to grow and cultivate their own foods—both plant and animal—was one of enormous importance in history. Until recently, the prevailing scholarly view was that early creative genius spread outward from clearly defined "hearths" of civilization and that agriculture's beginnings could be definitively pinpointed. But recent archaeological finds in the Americas and elsewhere make that hypothesis less certain. It seems more likely that the major human occupation of farming developed in many distinct locations, evolving in bits and pieces as the cultivation of plants and the domestication of animals was added to a hunting and food-gathering way of life.

There is no indication that prehistoric humans experimented with the domestication of plants and animals before the end of the last Ice Age, around 10,000 years ago. Until then, hunting and the gathering of wild plants were the sole food sources and the main occupations of humanity. Humans were restricted in territory to those locations where there was an abundance of game and wild plant food, and unable to establish permanent villages because of the need to follow the seasonal migrations of animals and the growing cycles of edible plants.

Both men and women played important roles in this subsistence economy. Men were responsible for the animal protein that hunting provided, while women ranged around the encampment gathering a wide variety of naturally growing plants, which served for both food and various domestic manufactures, such as cooking utensils and woven baskets. The same plant that served as part of an evening meal might also provide a dye for coloring or be used as a medicine. Women who were nursing children could not easily travel as widely as men, so they became intimately acquainted with the resources of the plant world and spent part of each day collecting plants.

The idea that these same wild food sources could be domesticated appears to have developed spontaneously in many different sections of the world. The evidence now available suggests that the Near East may have been the scene of the earliest agricultural experimentation. The evolution from *food-gatherer* and *hunter* to *farmer* was a gradual process, slowly taking place over generations as farming met with greater success and its harvest could provide a larger percentage of the food supply.

Hunting and gathering are still the main sources of food for the small number of truly primitive peoples left in the world. In addition, these techniques serve as sources of supplementary food for many other people in rural regions. Very often, these practices are now either linked with a sport such as hunting or a hobby such as wild-mushroom gathering. Gathering of food has also evolved into a commercial activity. Wild rice is harvested from the marshes of central North America by Native Americans and sold as a gourmet delicacy. In a similar fashion, the gathering of wild bird eggs from along the sea cliffs of England was a widely followed and profitable sideline until well into the 19th century. *Bee hunters*, who tracked their quarry through the forest to the hive and then seized the wild honey, have been active across the world from the dawn of history. The techniques of subduing bees and extracting honey used by the domestic *beekeeper* were originally the product of the hunter's observation.

In the hills surrounding the Fertile Crescent, including parts of Turkey, Iraq, and Iran, early inhabitants lived off the naturally growing major cereal grasses of wild wheat and barley, and hunted the sheep and goats native to the area. At some point, people found that it was easier to tend a flock of sheep near a campsite than it was to stalk them on the hillsides. It seems reasonable to assume that hunters brought home young animals, intending to keep them for a short while before slaughtering them, and found that they adapted easily to life at the camp. As it became clear that sheep and goats would not only live comfortably in close proximity to humans but would also breed and increase their numbers, the advantages of an assured food supply were obvious.

At approximately the same time, people began to experiment with the domestication of emmer wheat and barley. Flint sickles—tools with a short wooden handle topped by a sharp curved blade for cutting—were used as early as 10,000 B.C. in Jericho, in the Near East. It is possible that they were used for harvesting domesticated grain; they might just as plausibly have been employed in cutting grass for thatching and weaving. But it is unlikely that they were used for the harvesting of wild cereals. The wild wheat and barley native to the Fertile Crescent reproduce easily. The seeds (grain) are attached to the husk of the plant by brittle stems that will shake free in the slightest wind. Harvesting was a difficult affair for the food-gatherer, and care had to be

From the earliest days of farming, children have been employed to scare away birds that might eat the precious seeds. (From History of Egypt, *by Clara Erskine Clement, 1903)*

taken to break off the grain-bearing heads gently to retain the seeds. Even then, many of the brittlest stems would break and the seed would be lost.

When the first farmers began to collect and resow the seeds that they had harvested, they set in motion a developmental cycle that would lead to the abandonment of food-gathering as an important occupation and make farming predominant. Without necessarily intending to, they began to select out a high percentage of exceptional plants with tough stems, which could be harvested without the seeds being lost. As the seeds of these exceptionally tough plants were grown generation after generation, hybrids developed that did not readily give up their seeds and depended on human sowing for reproduction. This domesticated grain gave a much higher yield than its wild cousins and became increasingly prized.

The increased and dependable food supply that goats, sheep, and domesticated cereals provided made it possible to support large numbers of people and establish fixed farming villages. Growing populations in the hills of the Fertile Crescent found that lands ideally suited to a hunting and food-gathering culture were not as attractive to a herding and farming community. Settlers moved down from the hills into the fertile plains below, bringing their animals and bags of seeds with them.

At Ali Kosh, on the plains between the east bank of the Tigris River and the Zagros Mountains, a community grew up around 7500 B.C. that kept many goats and a few sheep brought from the higher mountain elevations. The earliest Ali Kosh inhabitants supplemented their animal protein with a vegetable diet that depended heavily on the gathering of wild alfalfa, wild oats, goosefoot, and other native plants. Cultivated cereals were only a minor portion of the diet, but the people did plant both emmer wheat and a two-hulled barley that were not native to the plains.

These farmers used a primitive slash-and-burn planting technique that in all essentials is still to be found in poor cultures, where human labor is the only affordable power source. First, the selected planting area was burned to clear it of its native plant life. This technique also served to enrich the soil with the ashes of the burnt vegetable matter. The farmer then used either a wooden digging stick or a wooden hoe to break up the earth and make it ready to receive seeds. Walking across the field, the farmer scattered the seeds carefully saved from the last harvest and tried to achieve an even distribution. The last step in planting was to turn loose a herd of goats or flock of sheep into the plot, driving them back and forth across the seedbed to trample the seeds into the earth, where they would be out of the reach of marauding birds or insects. Hand-weeding of undesirable plants was a continuous chore occupying the entire farming family.

If sufficient rain fell and no disasters interfered with the crop's progress, the cultivated wheat and barley were harvested in the field by the farming family, using flint sickles. The grains were then roasted to render the husks brittle so the seeds would separate. Once the grain had been separated, it was ground on limestone slabs for preparation into food. Many early village sites had storage pits, some with plastered walls, which were probably used for grain storage, providing a food supply during seasons when few naturally occurring food sources were available.

By 7000 B.C. the cultivation of emmer wheat, einkorn wheat, and barley was the major source of food for growing numbers of people living in farming villages throughout the Fertile Crescent. Domesticated sheep and goats were common, and both dogs and pigs were kept in at least one place, Cayonu in Anatolia. By 5000 B.C. farming had spread to become the dominant fact of life for civilized people in a wide area. In Crete, Cyprus, and Anatolia, farmers lived in villages and raised an increasing variety of foods, including bread wheat and lentils.

In Thessaly and Macedonia, the domestication of animals was the major occupation of the farmer. In addition to the ever-present sheep and goats, farmers undertook the large-scale domestication of two animals that would become fixtures on the agricultural scene. The heavily wooded areas of northern Greece had abundant big game, and among the most impressive specimens were the wild boar and the aurochs, a massive, long-horned wild cow. Farmers developed the domestic pig and cow from these game animals in much the same way that sheep and goats had been tamed, and they provided excellent food sources.

Agricultural stirrings were also felt elsewhere in the world by 7000 B.C., but did not lead into the massive change from nomadic gathering and hunting to settled farm village life until much later. Pumpkins and gourds were cultivated in northeastern Mexico, and in several parts of Central America plants such as avocados, chilies, and tepary beans—all of which were later widely cultivated—were already an important part of the diet.

At the Spirit Cave in northern Thailand, archaeological research strongly suggests that peas, beans, gourds, and water chestnuts may all have been planted and harvested. Still, small seasonal gardens, where experiments with cultivation were carried out, seemed to be the rule.

Once various animals were domesticated, herders and poulterers had to learn how to nurse them through illnesses. (From Harper's New Monthly Magazine)

In most of these areas outside of the Near East and Europe, farming as an occupation did not yet exist. Care of the gardens was probably undertaken by the women, who were directly in charge of the domestic maintenance of the encampment. The cultivation of small gardens of foodstuffs and herbs was a natural outgrowth of the food-gathering and preparation women had traditionally been largely responsible for. Gardening developed into a woman's specialty in most agrarian cultures. Gardens were planted next to the family dwelling, enabling close supervision and cultivation for the growing vegetables. While men have always gardened, their primary farming occupation has been field work, which demanded long hours of arduous labor away from the immediate home area. The physical work of the woman gardener could be equally taxing, but it could be scheduled around the demands of nursing infants, caring for young children, and domestic maintenance.

Primitive village farming traveled northward from Greece after about 4000 B.C. into central Europe, concentrating on the fertile plains of southern Hungary. One reason for the spread of farming cultures was undoubtedly the expanded population that agriculture made possible. Farmers could depend on a constant food supply and settle into villages, where food could be stored to ensure survival during times of need. The survival rate of children and adults rose rapidly as hunting and gathering were replaced by farming. As the villages grew, some families would move on to less crowded areas.

Another reason many farmers had to move on was the form of agriculture that they practiced. New fields opened up by slash-and-burn clearing would initially be very fertile. When the only tools available to the farmer to work the land were the digging stick or hoe, however, the land quickly began to lose its ability to retain moisture and fertility. After a few short years of cultivation the farmer's crops would diminish to such a point that the fields had to be left fallow to slowly regenerate themselves. Since this might take a decade or more, it was only a matter of time before the usable land in any one location was no longer sufficient for the needs of the

For thousands of years, farmers in North Africa and Western Asia used a shaduf *to help them irrigate their farm land. (From* History of Egypt, *by Clara Erskine Clement, 1903)*

growing farm families and a group would leave to colonize a new area.

From around 4000 B.C., farm villages proliferated throughout Europe. In many places the people also depended on hunting and gathering to supplement their diets, but along the rich farmland of the river valleys and plateaus in central Europe a distinct society of farmers called the Bandkeramik culture lived almost entirely by agriculture and animal breeding. They founded permanent settlements of 200 to 600 people throughout the region. The typical farm village consisted of 10 to 20 rectangular, gabled, wood-and-wicker longhouses, which could be as large as 40 meters long, though they were invariably only five or six meters wide. The village also had numerous storage buildings, and farmers commonly kept their livestock (mostly cattle and pigs) in a fenced enclosure circling the village, where they could be protected from predators.

In the land between the lower courses of the Tigris and Euphrates rivers, a colonizing group of Sumerians started intensive farming between about 4500 and 4000 B.C. Their earliest settlements were reed huts in the swamps surrounding the arms of the lower Euphrates, but the lure of the immensely fertile flood plains drew these early farmers to undertake land reclamation and irrigation, setting the stage for a revolutionary advance in both farming and civilization. In the primitive farming villages that were present throughout Europe and the Near East, all people worked at farming to support themselves; only a small portion of a farmer's time and effort went to labor done in the interest of the community as a whole. In contrast, as the Sumerian village farmers began to transform their new territory into productive farmland, a greater amount of cooperation was called for. Dikes had to be built to protect the land from the seasonal flooding of the rivers, and canals had to be dug to drain and irrigate the land. All of these constructions had to be constantly tended to prevent flood damage and silting, which might choke off the flow of water. Farmers had to look beyond their own private plots of land and allocate some of their time to this community responsibility.

The land was almost unbelievably fertile when it was irrigated, but it gave up its bounty only to people who were able to make long-range plans and create the means to exploit its wealth. Barley gave an enormous yield, but in a country that lacked both stone and metal, it could be harvested efficiently only after the invention of the ceramic sickle made from clay fired at 1200 ° F. Date palms provided a variety of useful products but they yielded fruit only after careful irrigation, artificial pollination, and a full five years of lead time from their first tending. Sumerian animal husbandry also displayed the same farsighted planning; careful breeding developed the first woolly sheep and goats, whose value extended beyond their role as meat and milk animals. Irrigation also permitted the establishment of fruit and vegetable farming on a large scale; cereals were joined by apples, grapes, plums, onions, and other tasty additions to the farmer's crops.

The farmer's greatly increased productivity owed much to irrigation, but some time before 3300 B.C. farmers in Sumer and nearby Egypt made another major technical advance in farming, which had a tremendous impact on the agricultural scene. Animals that had previously been used solely as sources of food (though wool was just being developed from sheep and goats) were put to work as beasts of burden. Wooden plows were invented, and drawn by oxen or asses to turn over the irrigated fields. The plow was much more efficient than the wooden digging stick or hoe that had previously been the farmer's sole tools. Farmers found that they could also harness the strength of animals to haul carts loaded with the harvest, making it possible to move large amounts of grain overland to a storage point or canalboat for further transport.

As Sumerian agriculture blossomed and irrigation constantly expanded the amount of land that could be farmed, farm villages grew into townships that were able to provide more centralized services. Farmers began to produce crop surpluses for the first time, and needed a means of profitably distributing them. Dividing up the all-important water in the irrigation system and maintaining that system also demanded a strong centralized control. By 3000 B.C., the Sumerian civilization based on agricultural prosperity had matured into a great nation of cities, whose inhabitants went out into the fields during the day to tend to the farms. The national wealth rested on the produce of the farmer, and an ancient Sumerian saga recounts how a king exported grain to Iran in exchange for precious metals and cut stone with which to erect a temple to his goddess. Religion played a central role in the farmer's life. Farmers prayed to a goddess of fertility and brought their surpluses to the temple grounds for storage.

As the civilization became affluent, a new system of farming developed. Valuable farms were owned by people who did not actually work the land themselves. The king, nobility, and temples owned vast estates, and farming became an occupation that employed *overseers, harvest supervisors, storehouse recorders,* and *work foremen,* as well as *field laborers,* who did the actual plowing, sowing, and reaping.

Individual farmers were still numerous, however, and they could anticipate a ready market for their surpluses, once they had brought them into the city's marketplace. Their profits would be limited, though, by the portion of the crop that would inevitably go for taxes; the portion that would be the temple's tithe; and the labor they would be required to do in the service of the state to help maintain the canal and irrigation system.

In the Nile valley of Egypt, farming did not become a major occupation until domesticated sheep, goats, and pigs were introduced from the Near East about 4000 years B.C. The earliest Egyptian village farms ran true to the Near Eastern model, growing barley, emmer wheat, and flax on high ground overlooking the Nile. By 3600 B.C. enterprising farmers had moved down from the dry heights to the flood plain of the river. They took full advantage of the annual flooding of the Nile; coming in October after the harvest was in, the floods spread a layer of fertile silt over the topsoil, making crop rotation and fertilization unnecessary. The farmers' fields emerged from the flood renewed and easily workable with little more than a wooden hoe, ready to receive another crop.

If the tilling of the soil was an easy chore for the Egyptian farmer, maintaining a growing system of dikes and canals to make full use of the flood was an annual time-consuming task. As the immensely productive fields provided growing wealth to Egypt, farmers became part of a complex and sophisticated social system. By 3000 B.C., when the country became unified under a ruler called a pharaoh, the farmer had to deal with an extensive government bureaucracy, which controlled agriculture throughout the kingdom.

Herders who accompany their flocks to mountains for summer grazing have always had a lonely life. (From Picturesque Palestine)

The Egyptian farmer's main crops were emmer, wheat and barley, serving to make bread and a barley beer. The phrase "barley and beer" was widely accepted as a synonym for wages of any kind, because these crops were the main sources of income in Egyptian civilization. Onions, lentils, flax, and beans were widely grown too. The Egyptians also turned their attention to the breeding of an ever-increasing number of domestic animals. In the swampy, untillable wetlands of the Nile, domesticated ducks and geese were raised for the table by farmers who occasionally depended on boats for transport as they tended their flocks. Drier areas, which were still of only marginal crop-raising value, supported huge herds of cattle, sheep, pigs, and goats; some wealthy owners numbered their animal assets in the thousands. Directed breeding of farm animals for specific qualities produced distinct strains of cattle for milk and meat; a specific breed of hunting dog; and even a sheep bred for its inordinately fat tail—so heavy that it had to be supported by a small cart drawn by the animal.

Much of the productive farmland and grazing land was owned by the pharaoh, temples, and other large land owners. The manual labor involved in farming provided the basis for the country's wealth, but the farmer had low status next to the growing hierarchy of *priests*, *nobles*, and *artisans* comprising Egypt's diversifying culture.

Tenant farming became the rule, with the farmer paying a fixed rent of three-and-a-half bushels of grain per acre for the use of the land worked. Farmers were no longer self-sufficient individuals, but relied on their *landlords* for seed corn and on the government for the maintenance and regulation of the all-important irrigation and flood control systems harnessing the Nile. Light wooden plows drawn by teams of oxen or asses were used to turn the land over, but the farmers rarely owned their own teams. Only wealthy landowners could afford such a luxury, and they either lent or hired out their equipment and teams to their tenant farmers. Some Egyptian plows incorporated a new device that made sowing a field a quicker operation. Attached to the plow was a funnel that dropped seeds directly into the opened furrow. A second plowing would sometimes be used to cover the seed, though many farmers continued to use sheep to trample the seeds into the earth.

Egyptian harvests were extremely productive, with the standard crop bringing a yield of 11 times the amount of seed sown. When the crop was ripe, the farmer harvested it with short-handled sickles still commonly made out of flint, though copper implements were being introduced into the country. The native stone was easy to work and cheap to use; and the farmer's sickle was a much easier tool to use with the new refinement of a curved handle, which allowed a more natural cutting motion. All during the harvest period, the farmer's children spent their days watching over the ripe grain, shouting to scare away quail and other feathered eaters.

On the large estates owned by the government or temples of the gods, mobile gangs of *laborers* were brought in to harvest the fields. These teams worked the country from the south to the north, migrating with the ripening crops. The *reapers* would use their sickles to cut the top of the plant; they would be followed by women who would pick overlooked heads and stray grains and collect them in bowls or baskets. Once this had been accomplished, the fields were cleared of the shocks, which were used to make straw. After sundown, women and children *gleaners* would scrounge for any over-looked scraps. It was customary at the end of the harvest for the reaper to be paid as much grain as he could harvest in one full day, a custom that continued for thousands of years in Egypt and would recur in many succeeding agricultural civilizations.

The harvested grain was threshed to separate the seeds from their husks by having cattle or asses tread on it in an enclosed area known as a threshing floor. Once this was done, the grain was winnowed to get rid of the separated chaff (husks); *winnowers*, often women, scooped up the grain with a curved wooden paddle and tossed it into the wind so the lighter husks would be blown away. The cleaned grain was gathered up and stored in large central silos, generally found on the temple's grounds. With the exception of the introduction of iron and steel tools, some Egyptian farmers on the flood banks of the Nile continue to use these techniques, basically unchanged from 3000 B.C.

A third great agriculture-based civilization arose in the Indus Valley on the Indian subcontinent. About 2000 years B.C., a civilization rivalling Egypt and Sumer was centered at Mohenjodaro and Harappa. Farmers supplied enough grain to fill granaries of 90,000 square feet, but little is known about the cultivation methods used to produce such massive surpluses. The Indians grew barley and wheat as their staple cereals, with dates, lentils, field peas, and sesame as supplemental crops. Indian farmers may well have used wooden digging sticks and worked fields periodically flooded by the Indus River in much the same way as the Egyptians worked the flood plains of the Nile, but no hard evidence has yet been found to support such a claim.

Around 1500 B.C. invading Aryans from the northwest conquered the Indian subcontinent. The new rulers were semi-nomadic warriors who shunned farming as menial work and required their conquered peoples to provide for them. The Indian concept of caste evolved after the Aryan takeover with four major distinctions based on occupation. The *brahmin* (priest), *ksattriya* (warrior), and *vaisaya* (merchant) were considered true Aryans and the ranking members of society. The farmer was relegated to the *shudra* caste as a subservient and powerless individual. This lowly status became an enduring Indian distinction; farmers who till the land themselves are still considered citizens of low status in much of India.

In the New World, the gradual development of maize (corn) as a crop plant, by around 3500 B.C. in Central America, was extremely important. Farming there was a rare occupation, practiced in only a few scattered village farm communities. Irrigation was apparently unknown, and farmers worked the land without the aid of the wheel (not known in the Americas until Europeans arrived in 1492) or the domesticated beast of burden.

By about 2500 B.C., farming had spread to northern China, where a dense and growing population of farm villages suddenly appeared in the vicinity of the Huang (Yellow) River. These farmers worked in a setting similar to that of their counterparts in Europe, growing millet and wheat as their main cereals and raising pigs, sheep, and cattle. The standard of living in a village was limited by the fertility of the fields around it and by the absence of advanced agricultural knowledge.

The semi-nomadic slash-and-burn economy in China gradually gave way to a settled farm village life during the reign of the Chou dynasty (1027-256 B.C.). A feudal state developed, which sharply distinguished between the upper classes and the peasant farmer's subservient role. An early Chinese saying explained how the differences between the two classes were seen: "The superior man uses his mind, the commoner his body. He who uses his mind rules, he who uses his body is ruled. He who rules feeds on others, he who is ruled feeds others."

Chinese agriculture followed the intensive farming pattern that had been pioneered in Egypt and Sumer, where state-administered irrigation systems required organized labor. The farmer existed as a serf bound to the lord's land and service during the early part of the Chou dynasty, but after the eighth century B.C. feudal bonds grew looser and independent family farms became commonplace. In about 500 B.C. iron plowshares were introduced into China, and deep plowing and tillage were added to the weeding, cultivating, spading, hoeing, and manuring that occupied the farmer's day. All farmers, whether bound to a lord or independent family operators, were subject to many obligations, in addition to the work their fields demanded. A portion of the harvest had to be paid as tax; a *corvée* (mandatory

As early as the Han period—roughly contemporary with Rome—the Chinese were using this type of treadle machine in winnowing grain. (From Thien Kung Khai Wu, *1637)*

labor for the government or lord) was customarily owed; and the farmer was liable to be plucked from the fields and pressed into service as a *soldier* whenever war erupted.

Farming in Greco-Roman Times

In the West, farmers worked the land as independent cultivators. Every estate in the expanding cultural region of the Greek Mediterranean measured its wealth by its vineyards and grain. Orchards and gardens flourished and received careful cultivation, manuring, and irrigation. For the most part, owners worked their own land and took care of all the tasks of the farm. Only the largest estates supported owners who did not actually farm but delegated the labor to slaves and hired hands. Farming was the occupation of almost everyone except the greatest nobles. Only the mobilization of the countryside for war could draw the farmer from the fields.

In Homer's *Odyssey*, set in Greece in the 13th century B.C., Odysseus boasts of his ability to reap and plow a straight furrow, even though slave *swineherds, goatherds, cattle breeders*, and *orchard keepers* run his estates. This practical knowledge was essential in a land where agriculture was a primitive and laborious occupation that provided the sole source of wealth. Every plot of land was divided into two breaks by the farmer, one to be sown and one to lie fallow; these were rotated each year to maintain the soil's fertility. Two or three plowings were done with the aid of a wooden plow drawn by a pair of oxen or mules. While most farming practices were primitive, *viniculture* (the raising of grapes for wine) became a highly specialized art practiced on almost every farm.

Greece entered the sixth century B.C. with an economy firmly based on farming, but a growing commercial and manufacturing trade was for the first time producing a new wealthy class of urban dwellers. Direct farming with the assistance of a slave or two was the rule on the small family farm, which still comprised the typical life-style. As an economy based on money developed, however, farmland that was valuable because of its location and fertility often came to be leased for a cash rental, with the landlord placing specific restrictions on its use and the maintenance the renter had to perform. Small farmers who were short on hard cash often fell prey to urban *moneylenders*, who charged high interest rates. Default (failure to repay a loan) meant the loss of a farmer's holdings to a creditor, who then became an absentee owner; such unfortunate farmers lost their personal freedom and became debt slaves. In Sparta, farming was completely turned into a servile occupation. All cultivation was done by *helots*, a conquered native people reduced to serfdom. Free citizens were forbidden by law from entering agriculture.

During the sixth and fifth century B.C. much of Italy was drained, and intensive farming began on the rich reclaimed soil around the mouth of the Tiber River. Even as Rome's power grew, it remained an agricultural society in which high status was given to farmers. Farming was considered the only occupation worthy of a Roman senator, though few would ever actually consider the prospect of personal labor on their land. The largest estates were called *latifundia* and were worked by thousands of slaves. The backbone of the Roman system, however, was the small and middle-sized holding worked directly by an independent farmer or run by slaves for an absentee owner.

Roman farming was a major topic of discussion and research for its leading citizens, depending as they did on their own farm holdings. In the early second century

Before the advent of mills, grain was often ground by hand like this, commonly by the women of the farm family. (British Library, by a 15th-century Persian artist)

B.C., Cato the Elder wrote a comprehensive treatise on farming that attempted to point the way to higher production for the average farmer and, in consequence, a stronger Roman state. Cato estimated that the typical 50-acre farm depending on olive oil production for its cash crop needed the following equipment: thirteen slaves, a foreman and his wife, five laborers, three plowmen, a donkey driver, a shepherd, and a swineherd; three teams of oxen for plowing; three donkeys with pack saddles to carry out manure; one donkey to power the farm's milling machinery; one hundred sheep; three big wagons; six plows and plowshares; yokes and harnesses for the farm's six oxen; one harrow; four manure hampers; four baskets; three pack saddles; three pads; tools of iron-shod wood, among them eight forks, eight hoes, five shovels, four spades, two four-toothed rakes for turning the manure pits that composted highly valued fertilizer, eight scythes, five straw hooks, five pruning hooks, three axes, three wedges, one hand mill; and presses for wine and oil. Cato also went to similar lengths to define the needs of a small vineyard and went extensively into agricultural theory.

Roman farming was a major and well-ordered industry that was carefully organized to show a profit. The Roman Senate continually sponsored analytical works similar to Cato's. Soils were analyzed and classified, as were different manures; pigeon droppings in particular were highly prized. The standards of Roman agriculture would remain, with only minor changes, the blueprint for subsequent European farming until the 19th century.

In Roman Egypt, where all land belonged to the king, the enormously fertile land of the Nile valley was worked by *royal farmers*, using the already time-honored methods developed under the pharaohs. Royal farmers were theoretically free citizens but were in actuality peasants strictly bound to the king's service. Since they were tenants, they had to pay rent and abide by royal land-use restrictions. Two-thirds of the land had to be given over to the production of grain, which was the basis

Wherever teams were hitched to plows, the farmer's labor was eased. (From Speculum Vitae Humanae, *by Rodericus Zamorensis, c. 1475)*

of Egypt's wealth as the supplier of grain for Rome. The state provided the seed, bought the harvest, and specified the manner in which the farmer could plant the fields.

More northerly Europe also supplied food to Rome, as the Empire expanded, but this was more often livestock than produce, for their lands were mostly forested. Enterprising farmers would drive their animals—cattle, lambs, pigs, even on occasion chickens and geese—to the cities, where they could find a ready market and a better price than in the country. These farmers, acting as *drovers*, would herd their livestock on paths alongside the main roads leading into the cities, setting a pattern that would exist wherever city populations supported such large-scale activity.

Across the world, the farmer's life in Han China during the third and second centuries B.C. was a difficult one. The techniques of legume farming (notably soybeans) and multicrop rotation to preserve the fertility of the soil increased the productivity of the typical small farm, but even in good years farmers had to turn to moneylenders to meet their tax and corvée burdens. A bad year marred by poor production or crop failure could be disastrous, forcing numerous independent farmers to sell their land to rich absentee owners and become tenants. Small farmers tilling fertile land near the capital were often displaced by rich investors who wanted their properties. This easily accessible farmland was valued at a full 100 times the price of equivalent frontier cropland. The perennial uncertainty of the harvest, the certain burden of taxes and operating expenses, and the pressure to sell out to developers gripped Han farmers in precisely the same way these factors continue to burden farmers throughout the world even today.

China's population rapidly increased during Han times and, as a result, farmers found their social status dramatically improved from their earlier treatment as scorned servants. Chinese emperors symbolically pushed a plow three times in the spring and actively promoted agriculture. The country's security depended on this change of heart, as a rush of people to the cities had brought on the prospect of massive food shortages in the empire. In 191 B.C. an imperial decree created an award to the *li-tien* (diligent cultivator), granting exemptions from taxes and the corvée and conferring both status and the official honor of rank to the productive farmer. The educated gentry and the mass of peasantry were still separated by strong class distinctions, but the social divide was one that could be crossed by upwardly mobile farmers.

The typical Han village farmstead was worked by an extended family consisting of several generations. Both women and men bore responsibility for the land's production, assisted either by hired laborers or occasional slave workers. The most precious crops were planted near the houses and tended by the village women. Vegetable gardens and orchards (often of mulberry trees) were the closest to the houses; beyond these were fields of textile plants such as hemp. These were the domain of the women farmers, who also were the village *weavers*. They rarely left this immediate area. Farther from the village center were the men's carefully tended fields of dry vegetables, and still farther were fields of cereal grains. At the bottom of the lowest-lying land, the men farmed terraced squares of rice. During the growing season, the male farmers often lived in cabins in fields far from their families. The peasant life developed during this time would remain basically unchanged until the transformation of modern China in the 20th century.

Farming in the Middle Ages

In the fifth century A.D. Rome's extensive and organized empire collapsed under the weight of barbarian invasions and its own internal decay. Vast areas of Europe that had been productively worked by both small farmers and the huge *latifundia* of the wealthy were abandoned when the commercial and protective benefits of the *Pax Romana* (Roman peace) were withdrawn. By the ninth and tenth centuries A.D., subsistence farming was once again the universal occupation of the West. Every person from the king to the lowest serf was tied to the land's production and lived in farming villages. Larger towns that were centers of commercial and industrial activity no longer existed to any notable degree.

As a feudal economy developed, the poor farmers scattered throughout the skeleton of the Roman Empire fell under the influence of rising local princes across Europe. Though much of Rome's legacy had been lost, the practice of taxation of the farmer's land was retained by the new nobility. Their *seigneural* system depended on taxation of the *manse*, which was descended from the Roman taxable unit. Each manse consisted of a dwelling and its allotted fields and was occupied by a family group that commonly consisted of several generations. The territory of the manse did not change and could be broken up only through its infrequent division into quarters or halves due to inheritance.

In the traditional pattern, the men are reaping and the woman is gleaning, gathering what is left. (British Museum, MS. Roy. 1 I IX, late 14th century)

Nearly all the land, from farmed manses to empty waste, was owned by lords or abbeys in great landed estates. The lords lived on their personal manses, called *demesnes*, which were far larger than the common peasant's land. The lord and those who lived with him in his manor depended on estate managers, or *stewards*, to keep them supplied with the ample food and drink that were the primary measures of a manor's wealth. Their food was partially supplied by the fixed tributes of eggs, coins, pigs, or sheep that were customarily owed by each manse under the lord's rule. A far cry from the commercial organization of the Roman farm, farming techniques in early medieval times degenerated to a primitive level that required many workers and was barely able to support those who lived off the land.

Lack of labor was a constant problem on the manorial lands. Slaves provided a partial solution, but during harvest and sowing, additional workers were needed. Hired hands were occasionally used, but the most common practice was for the lord to grant a plot of his land to a farm worker and his family in exchange for their labor on the lord's behalf. These newly created servile manses provided the manual labor pool of the demesne's land, and these peasant farmers were at the bottom of the manor's social ranking. Their obligation to the lord might involve a fixed task, such as taking complete responsibility for the working of a part of the demesne's land and turning over its entire production; or the manse's men might be subject to corvées, which took them away from their families to join work teams for the lord. They might be forced to neglect their own fields at critical times when the manor demanded help. Their jobs included planting, harvesting, or wielding mallets called *clodhoppers*, which were used to break up the soil after the plow had passed. If the lord saw fit, he could summon many of his servile farmers for "nights," which would remove them from home for an indefinite period of time to do his bidding.

A lord could also call on services from people on free manses, which had voluntarily attached themselves to the lord's territory in exchange for his protection and support. These were typically larger and wealthier than most peasant farmsteads. The free manses were able to support draft animals, and their obligation most often involved supplying a plow horse or cartage at specified times. *Plowmen* with their own teams were valuable individuals and were freed from much of the laborious, servile obligations of the poorer farmers who formed the manual labor pool. A definite social distance developed between the two classes of farmers, and friction between them was common.

In many cultures, the plowman had much higher status than other farm laborers. (British Library, by a 15th-century Persian artist)

The manse concept slowly became obsolete as the nobility found that it was more profitable to tax each individual dwelling instead of a whole locale. After the ninth century A.D. many farmers had an individual tax burden, but peasant families continued to live together in communal groups most often linked by family relationships, where several generations lived under one roof. Communities where friends had banded together as a brotherhood with communal obligations were also very common.

The nature of the land helped make close communal living the rule. Much of Europe was covered by dense forest or marshes where farmlands could be hacked out and maintained only by joint effort. The forests were valuable primarily as grazing lands for the pigs, which formed the meat staple of the medieval table, and solitary swineherds were among the sparse occupants of the uncleared lands. The medieval forest was measured by the number of pigs it could maintain on its forage of nuts. By 1050, substantial *assarting* (land clearing) had begun, as the population started to rise. In the 12th and 13th centuries, the large-scale assarting of forests and marshlands was continually financed by lords intent on creating rentable properties.

Communal peasant villages were formed on the cleared land, and a distinctive pattern of open-field farming became commonplace across Europe. Each farmer plowed long, narrow sections of land in the village's common planting area. There were no fences or markers to distinguish between individual plots, and each farmer ended up with a patchwork of small parcels scattered throughout the village fields, as inheritances broke up compact family holdings. By cheating on his plowing, a farmer could be a "devourer of furrows," adding to his land at the expense of his neighbor. This practice led to many disputes and was often denounced from the pulpit.

To maintain order, the communal village laid down strict rules binding its members and stubbornly resisted any attempts to change accepted practice. All furrows had to run in the same direction in the common fields, and the farmer had to abide by the village's customary pattern of crop rotation, sowing, harvesting, and cultivating. All animals went into a common village herd, which grazed on the waste and fallow land on a set pattern of rotation. Each farmer had to care for the common herd as his own when it was his turn to have the herd graze on his fallow fields. This involved extra labor on his part, but his land profited by the manure deposited by the grazing beasts, so the arrangement was fair. The only land that the farmer did not have to share was the enclosed garden and orchard area immediately surrounding the village.

The nobility depended on the peasant farm village for its wealth, but in the 11th and 12th centuries religious foundations rivaled them as landlords, acquiring huge amounts of land that they had inherited when the original owners died. In order to efficiently and profitably manage their holdings, the church leaders often would hire a special overseer for each manor called a *firmarius* (from which the word *farmer* derives). He was granted lifetime tenure as the head of the manor, exercising full power as the owner's agent. All agricultural dealings, from handling servile peasants to conducting the sowing and harvest, were his responsibility.

On the demesnes of the nobility, domestic servants formed the lord's *familia* and owed him personal loyalty and service. The *hayward* was a key person in the operation of the medieval manor in England. He was the general overseer and was responsible for a wide range of duties. He kept tally of the manor's seed and made sure that the customary obligations of produce and labor owed by tenants were met. The hayward also made certain that the enclosures around the manor's gardens and orchards were maintained, but his main task was the overseeing of the specialized and general laborers who formed the manor's work force.

During the spring, the highly valued plowmen—also called *bovarii* (ox drivers)—were the most important workers of the manor. The number of plows that a manor could support directly reflected its wealth. Plowmen had to be skilled in the yoking, driving, feeding, and doctoring of their teams. They had to be smart, skillful workers with knowledge about sowing, tillage, and the repair of broken plows and harrows as well. Plowmen received an exemption from normal taxes in exchange for their complete loyalty and skill. Each plowman was also commonly given a small cabin with garden land, free seed, and the use of the plow and team. As money came into general use, he also received relatively high wages.

Sowers were also important spring workers. Sowing required skill in order to make the maximum use of valuable seed. The sower walked down the plowed furrow at a fixed pace and threw handfuls of grain down at set intervals. Wet or dry ground required varying amounts of seed for maximum yield, so without changing his rhythm the sower would adjust the size of his handfuls accordingly. Seed was carried in a sowing basket or in a cloth wrapped around the sower's waist.

When harvest time approached the entire farm community of the manor went into action under the hayward's direction. Children took to the fields to bang noisemakers and protect the ripening corn from marauding birds. Teams of reapers were assembled, and the manor supplied work gloves to protect the men's hands from incapacitating blisters. The reaping team would begin at dawn and work until noon, when they would have an hour-long break. Reapers slept in the field during the noontime break and were brought bread, cheese, and barley beer by the women of the manor. Refreshed, the team would reap until seven p.m., stopping only for two 15-minute breaks for ale or harvest beer.

When the grain was brought in from the fields, it was moved to the threshing floor of the barn. One or two men using *flails* would suffice for small quantities of grain, but for the large harvests of the manor an eight- or ten-man threshing team was used. Holding the long arm of the flail, each man would hit the grain with the flail's free-swinging short arm. One man was the leader, calling the tempo and changes for the team. This was critical, as successful flail-threshing depended on a very rhythmical series of impacts, which shook the seed from its husk without directly beating and damaging it. (Flailing is still often used, when fine planting seed is sought.) Another reason why the team leader's expertise was important was that threshing could be a very dangerous business when 10 flails were slicing through the air. If a man fell out of rhythm, a cracked head was likely to result. A loose *sweple* (flail end) could also wreak havoc among the threshers.

The collection of the best seed for future use was a critical harvest occupation, entrusted to the farm women and children. The threshed corn was riddled by the women (a *riddle* was a sieve-like shaker) to finely clean the seed and separate out the chaff and other impurities. The riddled seed was then handpicked by children, whose small fingers were well-suited to the task.

Not all of the women active in the manor's farm production could be spared for extra harvest work. *Dairy maids* had their own year-round chores, which were independent of the harvest. Milking and the making of cheese and butter were almost exclusively women's occupations in manorial times and would continue to be so into the 20th century in many areas.

Not all farmland was directly controlled by the great manors and abbeys. *Allods* were free farms that sprang up around the edges of manorial lands, when the lord's slack management neglected to enforce his right to collect rent and tribute. After the passage of years of rent-free occupancy, the land was considered debt-free and independently held. Peasant farmers were constantly seeking to quietly carve out their own holdings free of manorial taxes and obligations, and to escape the notice of the estate's management. Once a farmer secured his freehold, he vigorously resisted subsequent attempts by the lord to tax him. By the 13th century, holders of allods were active village members and would unite to resist manorial pressure. The allod of the free farmer was threatened each time its holder died, however. Many allods became fragmented into small, unworkable parcels divided among a farmer's sons, and many more were donated to the church by a dying farmer seeking to ensure his heavenly future.

Although the allod was a free property, it was not an entirely independent one. It was subject to many pressures from the manor's preeminent feudal dominion. A peasant farmer might own his own land but still be subject to his lord as a loyal personal retainer. The lord was unquestioned war leader and dispenser of justice as well. The manor's economic might also dominated the allod. The demesne controlled the marketplace, was the employer of seasonal help, served as the broker for trade with outside buyers, and could provide aid and credit in hard times. The allod was subject to other pressures as well. Royal taxation and demands for goods or services, which varied with the strength of the current king, did not recognize the free peasant farmer's exemption.

Some farmers specialized in growing vines, doubling often as winemakers. (By Jost Amman, from The Book of Trades, *late 16th century)*

During the 13th and 14th centuries, a major economic change affected the lives of peasant farmers. Money became the common standard of value, and most of the best farmland had already been reclaimed from the forests and wastes of Europe. Population was up, and the value of the dependent farmer's manual labor was sharply diminished. Lords found that the cost of supporting a large permanent *familia* of dependent labor was greater than its value. By the 13th century, all peasant dues came to be collected in cash throughout most of Europe, and the corvée was no longer employed. The only full-time domestic laborers were the plowmen and *harrowers*, who broke up chunks of earth and leveled the ground after plowing. Sowers were hired when needed and paid in corn depending on the size of the seedbed. Women were hired in the springtime as *weeders* for a fixed daily pay. Reapers were hired at harvest time and were paid a percentage of the harvest; they were usually entitled to every 11th, 15th, or 20th sheaf.

The rising importance of money allowed nobles to live richly without having to exercise direct management of their land. *Share-cropping*, also called *metavage*, became an increasingly important arrangement, with the lord leasing out his property in return for a percentage of the harvest. The *sharecropper* was closely controlled as to the amount and variety of crops he could raise and was required to maintain his rented land. The typical peasant farmer had a meager existence under this arrangement. The family hut was furnished with a stick or two of furniture, an occasional pot, and a bed covering. The farmer's wealth was still measured in his flocks, even though coin was used to meet his obligations to the lord of the manor.

The demesne lands of the lord were also often leased out, as the noble family removed themselves to castles in more central locations. The operators of leased demesne land were generally upper-class farmers drawn from the clergy, the petty nobility, the bourgeoisie, and domestic officialdom. The rising profitability of taxable land for the nobility led them to finance *villeneuves*, new towns carved out of wild territory. In the Netherlands, extensive reclamation of sea bottom for farmland was taking place, and all across Europe farmers were attempting to till land that had been previously considered of little value. The confining bonds of personal service that had characterized earlier manorial farming were relaxing, and communal villages were flourishing and conducting active trade in local marketplaces. Specialized crops were readily marketable in the revived commercial world. English *bee masters*, for instance, saw their honey exported to the Continent and sold the beeswax from their carefully managed apiaries to *chandlers* (candlemakers).

The Black Death

The stable, relatively prosperous years of the early 14th century were soon rudely shattered. From 1314-1316, three years of disastrously bad weather resulted in almost universal crop failure, and widespread famine weakened many recently established farm communities. In 1347 the farmer's world was drastically altered, along with all of Europe, by the appearance of the Black Death. By the time the plague had run its course, one-third to one-half of the population of Europe had been killed. Villeneuves, allods, and assarts were abandoned as people fled to areas where the death toll was not as high. Even older-core farm villages were depopulated and suffered to fall into ruin. To add to the peasant's woes, wars raged throughout a decimated Europe and made the peaceful maintenance of a farm plot all but impossible, since farmers were likely to be forced to serve in the army or to feed any troops passing through the area.

In the aftermath of the 14th century's calamities, farmers found that their labor had once again become the most valuable commodity of an empty countryside. Lords who had become dependent on the income produced by their rural estates imposed higher taxes and enacted restrictive laws to make up for the wealth they had lost. The peasant farmer's freedom was limited in an attempt to continue the structure of an earlier society and to ensure a stable work force. In England, the Statute of Laborers passed in 1351 froze all wages at pre-plague levels and empowered landowners to seize and employ any vagrant healthy man, paying only a set rate. Additional reworkings of the statute added punishments of floggings and mutilation for farmworkers who attempted to leave the lord's land or resist his orders.

Similar restrictions were imposed across Europe, but they all proved useless in the face of the scarcity of labor and the willingness of desperate landlords to bid for workers regardless of the cost. The farmers, too, were unwilling to resubmit to servile bondage. Peasant rebellions broke out in many countries during the 14th century in response to new higher taxes and attempts to renew the corvée. In England, the great Peasant Rebellion of 1381, led by Wat Tyler, came very close to abolishing all feudal dues and services in exchange for an annual rent of fourpence an acre. Although the rebellion was crushed, the manorial system soon succumbed to the new economic conditions. Most farmers became rent-paying tenants with no further manorial obligations.

Along with the improved plow, farmers developed other devices to aid them in working ever larger fields. (From Diderot's Encyclopedia, *late 18th century)*

Attempts to restore the agricultural prosperity of the pre-plague years were only minimally successful. Many of the farmsteads staked out on marginal lands of forest and marsh were never reoccupied. In England, large landholders faced with a pressing labor shortage transformed much of their farmland to sheep-grazing acreage in an attempt to reap a quick profit. This move proved so successful that the enclosure of land that had formerly been shared by an entire community became a typical occurrence, even though there was considerable public outcry against the enclosure movement during the 16th and 17th centuries. The open-field system of a thousand years' duration changed, as hedgerows and fences sprang up to mark each farmer's land.

While farmers in Western Europe gained a good measure of independence as a result of the Black Death's reordering of society, their counterparts in Russia found that liberty was rapidly being withdrawn. Before to the agricultural recession of the 14th century, land ownership had been open to anyone in Russia regardless of rank, and the humble peasant farmer had had complete freedom to choose his home and move when it suited him. The recession made the Russian nobility determined to hang on to their peasantry and rents, and by the end of the 15th century a readily enforced ban had been placed on peasant movement except during specific weeks of the year. An exit fee was also required of farmers with little hard currency. The lords naturally became the sources of money lent to farmers at the same time that they raised taxes. As a result, many a free peasant farmer became a *kabala*, a debt slave bound in servile toil until the death of his noble creditor. Even the farmer who retained his freehold found restrictions, both legal and illegal, continually placed on his mobility.

By the 16th century huge numbers of runaways had left conditions that they found oppressive and tried to take advantage of their labor value as farmers on the open market. Lords with untilled fields engaged in fierce bidding wars to entice families of workers to come to their domains. Brazen labor kidnapping of entire villages of farming peasants was also a frequent occurrence. In response to these unsettled conditions, the Czar in 1581 declared a *forbidden year*, during which there could be no peasant movement. The restriction was intended to be a temporary response to a trying situation, but from 1603 on every year was a forbidden year, and the Russian farmer had been turned into a serf bound to the land of his master. Though peasant revolts from the 15th to the 17th century protested this virtual enslavement, they were all unsuccessful. Peasant farmers came under increasingly harsh control as they toiled on their fields, using techniques that would remain unchanged from the early Middle Ages to the 19th century. Their serfdom became indistinguishable from slavery and would remain in place until the Russian Revolution.

In Africa, Asia, and much of Europe the peasant farmer's world was unchanged by the passage of time. The daily life of the farmer remained fixed in the settled ritual of hand labor, rent and taxes, and a dependency on the vagaries of the weather. Families remained on the same small plots of land for centuries and took pride in

On the threshing floor, the wheat was separated from the chaff. (From Diderot's Encyclopedia, *late 18th century)*

upholding traditional techniques. The land was to be farmed only as it had been farmed in the past; the family's responsibility to the land and the community was to be only as it had always been.

Farming in North America

The settlement of North America transformed the farmer's status and foreshadowed the revolutionary changes in agriculture that would eventually sweep from the United States across the entire world. Feudal society, in which peasants labored in the service of their lord without hope of independent existence, did not thrive in the New World. Only the Dutch colony of New Amsterdam attempted to enforce this old system. Dutch *patroons* claimed huge landed estates in the Hudson Valley and were given rights similar to those of European lords. The farmers in the Dutch manors were all tenants, who owed annual rent in the form of produce and services to the estate. In return, they were able to set up farming with almost no capital and were given the right to cut wood anywhere on the manor. Although the rent was low, the pioneering farmer in a land of limitless timber, endless unsettled miles, and little government control was an unwilling tenant. Many simply took their families and "squatted" in an area removed from the landlord's direct supervision. An enterprising farmer could clear the virgin forest, plow a small acreage, and exist happily for years in denial of the weak authority of the patroon.

In the English colonies down the length of the Atlantic coastline, the first settlers were farmers by necessity, even though many had held other occupations in Europe. Upon arrival they immediately set up rude farmsteads, with little thought other than to harvest enough food to survive until the next season. Market agriculture would not develop until there were larger populations in the New World.

The prospect of settling in an entire continent of untold riches was a powerful inducement to a broad spectrum of immigrants from the cities and towns as well as the countryside of England. Land in the North American colonies was held by royally chartered companies such as the Virginia Company of London, which were eager to attract as many colonists as possible to clear the land, farm, and develop their investment. Settlers were granted parcels of land called *hundreds*. A *head-right* system developed, and spread from Virginia as far north as New York. In this system, each immigrant farmer received 50 acres of land for himself and 50 acres for each dependent.

The prospect of an immediate transformation from landless immigrant to freeholder of a massive (by European standards) estate attracted many families of settlers who were literate and middle class; they were a far cry from the peasant culture of closely restricted, tradition-bound farmers. The feudal practices of *entail*, which kept an estate from being subdivided by sale or inheritance, and *primogeniture*, which passed it intact to the eldest son, were both victims of the voyage to the New World. Mobility and free trade were the bywords of the new American farmers, and they quickly formed the dominant social class of a wilderness society.

The actual labor involved in setting up a farmstead in America was considerable, as the land had to be cleared of trees before it could be planted. Of the hundred or more acres the settler held, less than five would usually be transformed into arable land—land suitable for growing crops—planted roughly half in feed for the animals and half in vegetables for the table. Farming was the same round of plowing, sowing, weeding, reaping, and threshing practiced in Europe, but the farmer on a wilderness homestead also had to be alert against the attacks of hostile Native Americans and wild animals. Hunting provided an important source of food for the farm, and proficiency with a gun was a valuable addition to the farmer's survival skills.

At haying time, extra workers were brought in to reap the grain before it was damaged or spoiled. (From Diderot's Encyclopedia, *late 18th century)*

The land was planted yearly; little or no attention was given to the system of manuring, crop rotation, or fallow, which farmers in the small, long-settled countries of Europe had learned to employ. When crop yields began to decrease, a farm family would abandon the land and move farther into the unclaimed wilderness. An energetic farmer could boast of having worn out four or five farms during his lifetime. The land was limitless and open for the taking by any person with the will to clear it. As a result, American pioneers were markedly free of the farmer's traditional binding ties to a particular patch of soil.

In the Southern colonies, large plantations were established to raise rice and indigo for market, once the land had been initially settled. But the cultivation of both of these crops required intensive hand labor. In the absence of a group of peasants tied to the land, who would perform the labor, Southern plantation owners (like their counterparts in South and Central America) imported large numbers of slaves from Africa. These slaves experienced conditions far worse than the poorest serf in Russia, for they were forcibly removed from their homes, shipped in chains to an alien land, and sold to plantation owners. They did not even have the dubious benefit of being tied to the land, for—since they were treated as mere property—they could be sold and shipped to another plantation at the master's will, being torn once again from any new family ties they had developed in the New World.

Great areas were cleared and planted by slave farm laborers, who used the same hoe-and-spade techniques they had farmed with in Africa. White overseers acted as the agents for the plantation owners and were in charge of maintaining profitable production. The plantation system adapted to the introduction of cotton as the major crop of the region and would operate profitably for its owners until the Civil War.

At best, the slaves were treated as valuable tools for farming, akin to agricultural implements and livestock. At worst, they were totally at the mercy of overseers and masters, and could be whipped, maimed, or otherwise punished at will. They were kept in subjection and ignorance; few were allowed to learn even to read and write, and they were taught only such skills as would be useful to their masters. Not all slaves were treated harshly; a small number gained education and responsibility, and an even smaller number became free men, even before the Civil War. But for all slaves, the lack of freedom dominated their lives, and led many to try to escape to the North or to Canada. In the mid-19th century, as the idea of abolitionism grew, a frail network of escape routes called the Underground Railroad was established to help guide escaped slaves to freedom. Many fleeing across the country used the Big Dipper as their guide to the North Star, which kept them going in the right direction; that gave rise to the song, "Follow the Drinking Gourd." After the Civil War, these slaves were freed under the Emancipation Proclamation. They then had the right to move and establish new lives elsewhere. Many, however, remained tied to the land as poor tenant farmers and sharecroppers.

As the population of North America increased and towns became established, farmers across the colonies looked to sell their produce in order to earn money for the few necessities they did not manufacture for themselves. Most of the tools, utensils, furniture, clothing, and other goods that farmers needed were ingeniously fashioned from the native woods and plants by the farm family. In addition to possessing the ability to raise crops, the American farmer had to be a *carpenter*, *mechanic*, and jack of all trades.

The decision to bring a crop to market often brought all these skills into play, because of the almost total lack of roads or established freighting systems. Transportation in Colonial America was mostly by water, and most settlement followed the inland network of rivers. A farmer deciding to sell a harvest downriver at a town or fledgling city was first faced with the problem of con-

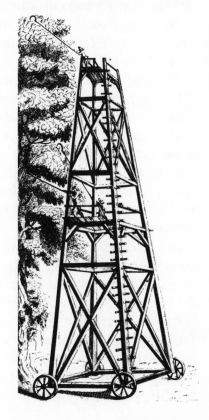

Structures like these were developed to allow workers to prune branches and pick fruit without damaging the trees. (From Diderot's Encyclopedia, *late 18th century)*

structing something able to carry the goods there. Timber from the farm's woodlot was felled and hewn, hauled by the farmer's team of animals—generally oxen—to the shore, and bound together to form a raft or flatboat. Barring accidents, the farmer-turned-boatman arrived at his destination intact and sold both his harvest and the lumber of the raft at a profit. The return home was on foot. The entire trip might take well over a month, during which time the farm was run by the rest of the family.

Where roads did exist, farmers drove herds of cattle, sheep, turkeys, pigs, and other livestock to market. Along the way were drover's hotels that provided rough accommodations for both herder and animals when darkness fell. On reaching their destination, farmers headed for the farmer's market, where they sold their herds to both dealers and individuals. Some of these drives covered great distances. During the 18th and 19th centuries, for example, farmers made large cattle drives from South Carolina to both Pennsylvania and New York City.

The increase in avenues of transportation during the 19th century opened new markets for the North American farmer. A network of canals, steamboat lines, and railroads made it possible for farmers to routinely raise crops destined for a distant marketplace, without having to personally escort them there. Farmers began to specialize, as urban marketplaces created demands for fresh vegetables and dairy products. Many farmers located near railheads or ports, where shipping was active, turned their production to *truck farming*, intensively planting relatively limited acreage in perishable crops that required quick distribution. By the middle of the 19th century, New York City was buying large quantities of fruits and vegetables from Southern farmers, and on a smaller scale its example was followed across the expanding nation.

Small farmers were able to show a profit on their holdings during years when no calamity of weather or natural disaster struck. With these profits, they could afford to buy the production of the rapidly expanding ironworks industry, which was turning out tools, plows, and assorted consumer goods in increasing supply. The United States was entering the industrial age, and the amazing inventive energy that characterized its industrial production was immediately applied to farm machinery that was bought by farmers across the country.

John Deere invented the steel-tipped cast iron plow in 1837, and it was widely used by the 1850s. Farmers whose production acreage had been limited by the amount of manual labor they could muster avidly accepted the assortment of newly invented farm machinery offered them. Between 1830 and 1860, mechanical threshers, McCormick's reaper, and mechanical seed drills were introduced and used on farms in many different sections of the country. Gang plows with numerous bottoms were pulled by the teams of horses or oxen that were still the heart of the farmer's stable. These advanced implements allowed ever-larger acreages to be tilled. Each year saw improvements in the mechanical arsenal. By 1855 a single man using a newly developed combine—which cut and threshed in a single operation—could harvest 12 acres of grain in a single day, an astounding increase in productivity.

Since North American farmers typically owned their own land and were able to cultivate only a fraction of the available acreage using traditional means, any device that could help them do more work was a profitable acquisition. In terms of the farmer's actual workday, agricultural machinery let a greater amount of work be accomplished with the same sunrise-to-sunset effort.

The Enclosure Movement

The situation was dramatically different in England, the only country outside North America to see significant mechanization in its agriculture and a change in the

Animals of all sorts were housed around the farmyard, including doves in the dovecote, the round tower. (From Diderot's Encyclopedia, *late 18th century)*

traditional farming practices that had been set in medieval times. The introduction of mechanical threshing machines in England led to a farm worker's rebellion in 1830. Angry farm laborers destroyed many of the newly introduced threshers and demanded higher wages from their employers. The uprising was decisively crushed by the government and its participants were imprisoned or deported, but it served to highlight conditions that threatened the existence of the common English farmer.

The life of the English yeoman (small landowner) had been irretrievably altered by the massive expansion of manufacturing and commerce that began in the late 18th century. Small, largely subsistence farmers had been the mainstay of a largely rural population until the rapid industrialization of the cities and the national economy. The growing population centers of the cities needed a more efficient food supply than the scattered patchwork of small holdings could readily supply, so the ruling gentry decided that the most profitable and workable course would be to create large farms by embarking upon a policy of *enclosure*. By petitioning for enclosure, a wealthy proprietor could establish ownership of a large area of land that was technically unimproved waste. Though undeveloped, the waste was hardly valueless or unclaimed. The common peasant farmers of England had held time-honored rights that allowed them to pasture their animals, cut wood, and farm small plots in the common waste. These traditional rights were often the keystone to the economic survival of poor, marginally self-sufficient farmers. It allowed them to raise a few animals for market and earn enough money to meet their bills. Stripped of access to the common land, the once independent yeoman farmer was faced with the prospect of becoming a hired laborer on one of the newly created large farms or migrating to one of the cities and entering into factory work. A steadily increasing number of men and women were forced to leave their now unfarmable small holdings and break centuries of family tenure as farmers.

The new enclosure movement marked an abandonment of the high value England had traditionally placed upon having a stable, independent farm population. Enclosure had been sporadically invoked since the 15th century, when a mania for sheep raising had taken hold of the gentry, but by the reign of George III at the end of the 18th century only 200 to 300 enclosure acts had been passed. The government had also insisted, by passing the Smallholdings Act of 1597, that all farm laborers' cottages had to have at least four acres of land attached to them for their occupant's use. This was repealed in 1775, and by 1800 some 3,500 acts of enclosure had ended the era of the smallholder's prosperity.

The change from family farmer to hired laborer was traumatic. The 19th-century farm worker's life was an uncomfortable and unhealthy one. Only plowmen, shepherds, and cowmen were supplied with housing on the farm itself, because of the value and nature of their duties. The common laborer was forced to maintain his own cottage, often miles from the farm and invariably damp and sparsely furnished. A one-quarter-acre garden plot now provided vegetables, in contrast to the farmer's former four-acre smallholding. Bad water, poor nourishment, scanty sanitation, and exposure to the elements endangered the health of the farm laborer's family. Tuberculosis, rheumatism, and childhood epidemics were rampant.

The farm worker had to provide his own scythe and other tools and was expected to put in a 6 a.m.-to-6 p.m. workday under the direction of the farm manager. Women were often hired as laborers and worked at the same jobs that the men did, but they were paid substantially less and worked a shorter 8 a.m.-to-4 p.m. shift in the fields, so they would be able to care for their children and cook meals. The shorter farm shift hardly meant a shorter workday. The farm woman often spent long hours augmenting the family's meager income by sewing piecework for a manufacturer during every spare moment.

Agricultural gangs of women and children were commonly hired as additions to the large farm's labor force. Assembled by an independent jobber called a *gang-master*, they were hired out on a temporary basis to any landlord who wanted a quick job done by workers he did not have to take any responsibility for. The effect of this scantily paid migrant existence of strenuous toil on the women and children of the gangs was ruinous and became a national scandal. After 1867 children under the age of eight were forbidden employment as farm workers, and women were not allowed to be part of an agricultural gang unless an officially licensed *gang-mistress* was present.

Many workers had long associations with a particular farm, but others were hired each year at fall hiring fairs held in the regional market towns. The farm owner, or more likely the hired manager, would survey the gathering of potential employees and hire on the work force for the next year. The skills of the workers present were easily distinguishable by the identifying emblems they wore in their hats: a piece of whipcord denoted the plowman; a flutter of wool the shepherd; and a small bunch of cow hair the cowman.

As a labor-saving agricultural machinery was introduced on the limited arable land of the English farm, farm workers found themselves unemployed as their services were suddenly unnecessary. By the end of the 19th century the number of workers leaving the occupation of farming had grown tremendously. A nation that had been predominantly agricultural in the 18th century counted only 25 percent of its male population in agricultural employment by 1851. Fifty years later a scant 12 percent were still farming. Many farmers

On ranches, shearers were employed to cut the wool from sheep and roll it for later working. (By W. H. Pyne, from Picturesque Views of Rural Occupations in Early Nineteenth-Century England)

emigrated not only to the United States but also to Canada, New Zealand, and Australia, where there was still an abundance of land. They sailed away in quest of a goal that was rapidly becoming unattainable in modern England: a freeholding for themselves and their families.

Belated efforts were made to preserve the farming class in England. During the last quarter of the 19th century, acts were passed to protect the health of farm workers by regulating the operation of dangerous farm machinery. In 1900 the Workman's Compensation Act was amended to include agricultural laborers in its coverage. Voluntary schemes were promoted by individual wealthy landowners and churches to allot small parcels of land to worthy farm workers in an attempt to recreate the smallholding, but these were statistically insignificant. All in all, little was done to reduce the abandonment of farming as an occupation in England, and by the 20th century the class of yeoman farmers had largely ceased to exist.

Modern Farming

England was the only European country where massive industrialization and a disregard for the survival of the individual farmer largely brought about the end of the family farm in the 19th century. Countries such as France, Belgium, and Germany retained a great number of smallholdings. Denmark moved aggressively to maintain its rural farming class. In 1769 the Danes passed a law forbidding the incorporation of peasant lands into larger estates. This protected the small farmer and set the tone for subsequent legislation, which stood in glaring contrast to Britain's enclosure laws. In 1899 an allotment act was passed, which enabled the small farmer to purchase from five or seven acres with the aid of a low-interest, 90 percent state-financed loan. As a result of these policies, Denmark's farm population remained vital, in spite of the pressures of emigration to the United States and Canada and a steady stream of rural people to the cities.

In North America farmers also came under economic pressure in the second half of the 19th century. They found themselves hurting because of high tariffs, railway freight charges, a fall in commodity prices, and a rise in interest rates. To help solve their problems, American farmers organized in a movement called the Grange. Initially envisioned as a largely educational association, the Grange had been founded in 1867 to advance the social needs of farm life. But it attracted thousands of new members from 1873-1874, with membership rising to 800,000.

The Grange movement quickly changed its focus and became an active marketing and farmer-support system, which had as its basic motive the elimination of middlemen in both the sale of the farmers' products and the purchase of manufactured items for the farm. Local Granges sold a wide array of products—ranging from shoes to threshing machines—to their members. Ambitious local associations bought many warehouses, grain elevators, and even steamboat lines in an attempt to control their own distribution systems.

There was not enough organizational expertise among member farmers to cope with the rapid expansion of the movement, however, and by 1876 the Grange had fallen into disarray. But the ordinary farmer's stance as a member of a political and economic community was well-established and resurfaced in the Farmer's Alliance of the 1880s, which developed a radical political program. The Farmer's Alliance advocated a host of economic and cultural changes, including a call for the free coinage of silver, an eight-hour workday, and government ownership of railroads and utilities.

During the 1890s farmers in the United States could look beyond the boundaries of their fields and take pride in their membership in a massive and well-represented group of voters forming the Populist Party. The voting strength that farmers demonstrated in state legislatures across the country spurred the government to enact a substantial body of law that directly affected the farmer's daily life. Rural traveling libraries, farmer's institutes, schools, and rural free mail delivery all brought the family out of the isolation of the country farmstead, which had stifled educational advancement.

A thriving agricultural press, exhibition, and college research network was established, as well as the U.S. Department of Agriculture. The farm operator was then able to keep up with the continual flood of technical development that was producing more efficient machinery, feed, seed, and marketing strategies. Though it was not immediately apparent, this network of information and technical assistance would gradually work to make the practice of farming too complex and expensive for the small operator by the middle of the 20th century, paradoxically hurting many of the same people it was set up to aid.

The rangeland of the western United States was too dry for intensive cultivation, but *ranchers* found that this land readily supported huge herds of cattle. *Cowboys* earned their livings working as hired hands on large ranches or by running small spreads of their own. The cowboy's work was largely done on horseback, often involving trips of days or weeks away from the settled existence of the ranch house complex. Cowboys rode across the open rangeland checking on the stock or seasonally driving herds to different pasturages. Bedrolls and food packed on the horse's saddle formed the working cowboy's equipment, and his job took him into whatever weather the unsheltered outdoors had to offer. The cowboy's counterparts in Latin American countries of similar climate and terrain were often called *vaqueros* or *gauchos*.

Profit from ranching operations was realized by the sale of cattle to buyers, who shipped the animals eastward to the major slaughterhouses in urban areas. Annual cattle drives sent thousands of cattle hundreds

of miles from interior ranching sections to the main lines of the transcontinental railroads. Famous routes like the Chisholm Trail were used in cattle drives after the Civil War. *Trail bosses* directed the operation, overseeing the small crew of cowboys working as *drovers*, who kept the herds intact and moving.

Sheepherding began to rival cattle ranching as a major user of the open rangeland of the American West during the last quarter of the 19th century. Competing cattle and sheep interests met in bitter, often bloody confrontations. Sheep graze differently from cattle, cropping

On plantations in America's South, slaves picked crops, work now done on large farms largely by migrant laborers. (From Author's archives)

plants more closely to the ground and making it difficult for cattle to survive on the same land. Cattle ranchers rejected the introduction of sheep into the open rangeland that had been their exclusive domain.

Killers, such as Billy the Kid, were sometimes hired by the cattle ranchers in a last-ditch attempt to save their rangelands, but by the late 1880s the scene had irrevocably changed. Extensive fencing with barbed wire closed many of the traditional cattle drive routes, and the construction of feeder railroad lines made long overland trips unnecessary. Cowboys remained on their ranches, and "riding fence"—a constant round of patrol and repair—became a standard part of the job. Today, ranches still employ cowboys in very similar positions, though four-wheel-drive pickup trucks are sometimes used to supplement horseback patrols.

The expansion of colonial empires in the 18th and 19th centuries dramatically affected farmers in land brought under foreign rule. Subsistence farming and long-established local agricultural patterns were rarely those that provided the highest profits to the colonial overlords. Decisions made in Western capitals transformed the lives of hundreds of thousands of farmers in regions such as India, Indonesia, Central and South America, and Africa.

In order to efficiently grow and harvest valuable crops such as tea, rubber, coffee, and cotton, vast territories were cleared and organized into plantations run by European *farm managers*. Laborers—whose former occupations had largely been family subsistence farming of small varied plots of vegetables—were pressed into service on the plantation work forces in conditions of actual or effective slavery. Their movement was restricted and their daily working lives controlled by *overseers* empowered to flog (beat) or otherwise punish them. The harvest of the plantation's crop did not at all enrich the workers who raised it.

The breakup of the major colonial empires in the aftermath of World War II ended some of the worst cases of farm labor exploitation, but in many countries the lucrative and established plantation system was basically unaltered and remained in the hands of a small class of wealthy owners. Laborers now often have some freedom of movement and receive nominal pay, but in many developing nations they are still held in economic serfdom by the plantation's owners.

In other parts of the world, agricultural production did not increase dramatically. In Japan, however, a rising population forced the nation's farmers to make more efficient use of the very limited amount of arable land available. Farms of only two to five acres were the norm, and these were often made up of a scattered collection of small lots that did not border each other. The peasant farmers of the country had lives that were sharply limited by the tiny acreages available for their use.

In the 17th century the country had been unified in a feudal state, and the tenant peasant farmers making up most of the population had been bound to their land and heavily taxed. Throughout the 18th and 19th centuries continuous rebellions and protests by the peasantry unsuccessfully sought relief from this situation. Serfdom was abolished in 1868, when the Meiji Restoration assumed control, but tenant farmers saw no real

Drovers herded sheep, oxen and other animals along special pathways, between seasonal pastures or on their way to market. (By W. H. Pyne, from Picturesque Views of Rural Occupations in Early Nineteenth-Century England)

difference in their lives. Rigid social classes continued to dominate Japan's culture, and tenants were at the bottom of the hierarchy. They still had to enter through a separate door and kneel whenever they came to the landlord's house.

In spite of their lowly position, Japanese farmers steadily improved their standard of living, increasing the tiny farm's productivity through ever-more-diligent and time-consuming attention to hand-weeding, fertilization, cultivation, transplantation of seedlings, and the like. Lacking any access to machinery, the Japanese farmer's massive investment of personal labor met the nation's demand for food and allowed their own families to eat tolerably well and purchase a broad range of household goods.

By 1920, the increasingly prosperous Japanese state acted to aid its farmers by making loans available and instituting price supports, because it realized how important their well-being was to the national economy. The first national peasant's union was formed in 1922, and by 1935 two out of every three farmers were members of agricultural cooperatives. Machines remained totally unavailable, however, until after World War II.

Farming in the 20th Century

The 20th century brought enormous changes in the lives of farmers across the world, though it would take 60 or 70 years for the technical advances pioneered in the United States to reach some parts of the Third World. Meanwhile the growing network of agricultural societies, colleges, and cooperative movements continued to bring the farm family out of the rural isolation that had traditionally kept their lives bound to unchanging patterns of grueling physical labor.

The key to the prosperity of North American farmers lay in the increasing use of machines that had resulted from the Industrial Revolution of the late 19th century.

The major innovation for the farmer, as well as the general population, was the invention of the internal combustion engine. Tractors powered by steam had been periodically tried out during the late 19th century as replacements for animal power on the farm, but they had remained an experimental and unsatisfactory device. Steam tractors were enormously heavy and inefficient; their use by the ordinary small farmer was unthinkable. In 1892, the first gasoline-powered tractor was started up, and the ensuing progress of rugged, hardworking farm machines would dramatically alter the day-to-day existence of the typical farmer.

The advantages of a gas-powered tractor were vastly attractive to the farmer. In addition to speedy plowing and cultivating, the tractor's replacement of the horse, mule, and ox as the farm's heavy hauler meant that substantial acreage tied up in feed could now be planted in marketable crops. The tractor also meant tremendous labor-saving for the entire farm family, because its mobile power plant could be easily adapted to the completion of many time-consuming and difficult chores. Tractor-powered saws, pumps, loading equipment, milling machinery, and an ever-increasing host of other useful devices made farm life easier. Farmer acceptance of the new-fangled invention was most advanced in the United States, where large acreages and an eagerness for new machinery were part of the agricultural history. In 1907 there were only 600 gas-powered tractors in the country; 13 years later there were 264,000. By 1940 more than a million and a half tractors were helping farmers raise crops—even though they still were missing from more than half of the farms in the United States. In other nations, with the exception of a handful of industrialized countries, tractors were unknown.

Peasant farmers in Europe were indirectly touched by industrialization. They found that their traditional smallholdings, where they worked hard with their own hands to make a living, were under heavy attack from a new class of business-minded large landholders. Land,

Though these women formed a farm labor union in 1936 in Kansas, many farm workers, especially migrants, have little or no organized protection. (By Arthur Rothstein, from The Depression Years, *Dover, 1978)*

rents, and labor were reduced to commodities on the landlord's ledgers and ruthlessly managed with the sole interest of turning the highest profit. Millions of families emigrated from Europe to the United States and Canada, seeking land of their own. Those who came during the early part of that massive exodus in the late 19th century were able to acquire land in the still unsettled Western plains. There, they were able to establish pioneering farmsteads at the cost of tremendous labor. Later peasant immigrants found it more difficult to establish farms in the United States because by then the best land had already been claimed. Farming was also somewhat in decline, as some of the rural population had begun to migrate to the cities.

Rural electrification brought great benefits to farmers around the world. Fledgling electric companies had rushed into service in the densely settled areas of North America, but sparsely populated farm areas were at first shunned by commercial investors as an unprofitable wasteland. Nations with a developing industrial base and farmers who were aware of the benefits of modernization found ways to overcome this obstacle. The earliest rural electrification programs were begun by farmers' cooperatives in Germany and Japan at the turn of the century. By 1920 it had become clear to the governments of technically advanced nations throughout the world that bringing electricity to the farm was an important national priority, because it would greatly increase farm production. Government programs subsidized power networks designed to bring electricity to farmers and other rural citizens.

The rapid advances of farm technology made crop yields rise dramatically for those farmers able to afford the investment of money needed to equip their holdings with tractors, mechanical milkers, combines, and the like. Even farmers with the best equipment, however, still faced traditional enemies—bad weather, insects, and disease—that could destroy their profits. In addition, farmers were not immune to the man-made calamities and social transformations that shook their countries. In Europe, the devastating effects of World War I on national economies destroyed many farmers' lands and livelihoods.

In Russia, the early 20th-century Communist rise to power had far-reaching consequences for the millions of peasant farmers touched by it. During 1928-1929, the ruling Communist Party implemented a "revolution from above" on the populace. In one massive, jarring dislocation of past practices, peasants and their families were forced to join large collective farms whose administration was part of an ambitious national five-year plan to industrialize the Soviet economy. The abruptness of the changeover triggered widespread suffering and confusion, as crop yields declined and food shortages grew acute.

The revolutionary change in the Russian farmer's status endured in spite of the turmoil, however. The state guaranteed food, shelter, clothing, and medical care to a farming class that had previously been treated as degraded slaves at the mercy of large landholders. For the first time the peasant farmer enjoyed security (although during the early years it was not very substantial) and a respectable status as a producing citizen.

In the United States, the onset of the Great Depression in 1929, coupled with a prolonged drought across the midsection of the country, accelerated the trend away from the farm. This trend had been evident since the beginning of massive industrialization in the late 19th century. Small family farmers, whose agricultural roots spanned generations, were foreclosed off their land or forced to move as they watched the topsoil blown off their fields in howling dust storms. Many "Okies"—from the hard-hit dust bowl of Oklahoma—ended up moving to California in search of agricultural employment; they often became *migrant farm workers*, who followed the harvest of one crop after another as they traveled up and down the coast. Migrants had a desperately poor and uncertain existence during the Depression, but their lot was really a continuation of a pattern of exploitation that had long been commonplace on larger farms.

As mechanization had begun to make the farming of large acreages possible and profitable in the United States during the 1870s, the large population of Chinese immigrants was seized upon by the agricultural community for the hand-harvesting of fruits and vegetables—necessary to avoid bruising. By the 1880s Japanese immigrants had become the newest and most degraded class of farm worker, barely paid, maltreated, and discarded at will. Succeeding waves of Mexican and Filipino immigrants later provided a continuing source of cheap and undemanding labor for the large farmers. The plight of the Okie migrant workers was exceptional mostly because they had once been self-sufficient farmers.

Today, migrants are still an impoverished underclass of the American farm scene, whose ranks are filled largely by illegal immigrants from Mexico and the Caribbean. The daily routine of the migrant worker is one of hard manual labor for small pay. Some families have regular stops that they make as they follow a seasonal harvesting route from south to north. For the few weeks of their stay at any one location, migrants are often provided with barracks-like accommodations near fields or orchards. Other migrants camp near regional hiring centers and gather at the local Farm Placement center or similar office at 4 a.m., lining up in the street. Buses sent by the owners of large farms quickly pull up, overseers yell out the job and pay rate to the waiting migrants, and then they load as many workers as they need that day. By 7 a.m. hiring for the day is over.

The modern era of farming began after the end of World War II and radically changed the basic nature of farming and the role of the farmer. In the United States, electrification and the use of tractors became universal. Also, farmers possessed an effective weapon against insects for the first time, as a chemical arsenal including DDT and other pesticides became available. These would eventually cause problems of their own. Still, specially rigged airplanes flown by *cropdusters* continue to routinely spray insect-destroying chemicals during the growing season.

Other improvements came about as a result of the careful study of plant and animal genetics fostered by the network of agricultural colleges and societies. This work began to yield a growing number of hybrid crops that combined greater yields with disease resistance and superior market qualities. The farmer's herds also showed dramatic improvements as the use of artificial insemination with sperm selected from prize stock became commonplace. Another advance was the use of newly developed chemical fertilizers that were inexpensive and enormously increased harvests.

The proper use of this cornucopia of new technology and research required skills that many small farmers did not possess. Foremost among the skills needed was effective money management, since the amount of capital

This photograph may have been staged against the Dallas skyline in 1945, but it does speak the end of an era. (By William Langley, Library of Congress)

invested in machinery, land, buildings, seed, and livestock routinely ran into several hundred thousand dollars. Most of this wealth existed solely on paper. Everything that the farmer made was immediately put back into the farm or used to pay back the loans regularly taken out to finance the planting of the next year's crop.

The difference between a profitable year and a disastrous one hinged on the weather and on the prices reigning in the commodities marketplace. Ironically, the enormous increase in farm production threatened to destroy the farmer's ability to make a living, because of the resulting low prices for crops and livestock. To help the farmer survive, a series of government subsidies were enacted, which established artificially set minimum prices for farm commodities.

The number of small farmers in the United States dropped constantly as the costs of maintaining a modern competitive operation relying on machinery, pesticides, and fertilizer rose. Many farmers found themselves in the position of having a paper worth $500,000 or more in land and equipment—while they were struggling to break even year to year. The skyrocketing value of land in many areas also pressed the farmer. The potentially massive profits that could be reaped by selling off cropland or pasture persuaded many farmers to leave agriculture and break up family farms held for generations. The enormously potent traditional link between the farmer and the land began to shatter. Successful farmers became well-informed *managers*, who spent diminishing amounts of time actually attending to the physical labor of running the farm. Computerization of many farm decisions began to be widely implemented during the late 1970s, and the successful farmer of even a moderate acreage was often aided by a college degree.

In the late 1960s a breakthrough in plant development combined with improved fertilizers and pesticides had created an instant and unprecedented two- to threefold increase in wheat, rice, and other grain production. New varieties of plants and modern farming techniques were widely exported from the United States to under-developed Third World nations, where farmers' lives had been unchanged for thousands of years. This *Green Revolution* affected millions of subsistence farmers in cultures across the world, introducing machinery and miraculously prolific new crops that, for the first time, held a promise of a life removed from the raw edge of starvation.

For the hundreds of millions of peasant farmers living in China, revolutionary change came from another source. The farmer in old China had led an extremely precarious and circumscribed existence. Bound to traditional techniques thousands of years old, farmers found starvation, disease, and natural disasters very real and everpresent facts of life. The country's arable land was controlled by a very small landlord class, and the farmer had little hope of any advancement or improvement of his condition.

In 1949, the Communist Chinese victory irrevocably shattered the ancient structure of class society and private ownership of land. The peasant farmer moved through a carefully planned progression in education and ideology (political beliefs), which was based on the Russian example. The first step was the redistribution of the land, giving it to the peasant tiller who worked it. Next, mutual aid groups of six to fifteen households were set up, to band the farmers together in an agricultural cooperative, sharing certain machinery, expertise, and resources while retaining private ownership of their own plots. The result was constant friction over who would have use of the co-op tractor and other resources first; the solution was inevitably the formation of the advanced farmer's co-op, where all land passed out of private hands and became part of the collective. Irrigation, mechanized plowing, and the like became group activities planned by group decision-making. Six or seven co-ops often joined together to form a *commune*. The commune brought a stability and structure to the Chinese farmer's life, which had not existed for many centuries.

Modern agriculture employs a vast number of specialized workers. The self-sufficient generalist smallholder is rapidly disappearing in every country that is coming into the highly technological modern era. In the United States, about 60 percent of all farmers raise crops; the rest raise hogs, cattle, poultry, and sheep. Farmers are generally classified by the crops they grow or the livestock they raise. *Orchardists* grow fruits, such

Loggers, like these felling cedars in Lebanon, had been working in the woods for thousands of years. (From The Pictorial Sunday Book)

as apples, oranges, and cherries; while *dairyfarmers* raise cattle and market their milk. *Aquaculturists* manage carefully controlled bodies of water, raising products like catfish, trout, and oysters for sale as their main source of income. Such *fish farms* have been operated for thousands of years, straddling the border between farming and fishing.

Some specialists also operate *tree farms*. From the days when the famous cedars of Lebanon were cut down to build palaces for King Solomon of Israel and the great pharaohs of Egypt, *woodcutters* have been cutting down trees in forests around the world. Egypt and Mesopotamia had no forests of their own, and a profitable trade developed thousands of years before Christ, in which wood was brought from Lebanon and India to serve these high civilizations. Woodcutters have been found in every region of the world that has sizable stands of timber used for fuel or lumber. In most cultures throughout the centuries, lumbering has been a subsistence occupation requiring heavy manual labor with hand axes and providing very little economic return.

To meet the demand for wood over the centuries, woodcutters have laid waste to vast tracts around the world. Only in modern times, as both demand and knowledge of conservation have increased, have there been concerted attempts to replant such areas for future reaping. *Foresters*, employed either by private concerns or the government, manage woodlots, planning their harvesting and reseeding to produce an optimum return and maintain a renewable natural resource.

The work of foresters has become especially important in modern times. Commercial lumbering on a large scale came into its own during the 19th century, as a result of growing populations, rapid mechanization, and the appearance of superior transportation networks. Increased demand and the technological ability to process enormous amounts of lumber products made the financial incentives for major exploitation great.

These loggers were so proud of their trade that they staged a special exhibition of their work in Michigan in 1893. (Library of Congress)

Foresters like this one assess the size and health of woodlands under their care. (By Louisiana-Pacific Corp., from Society of American Foresters)

In North America, the vast stands of timber and America's phenomenal growth led to a mechanized industry that depended on steam engines for the transport and processing of huge volumes of wood. *Lumberjacks*—their work spawning tales of legendary strength—lived in logging camps set up in the woods near the stand of lumber to be harvested. *Fellers* were the elite workers in the camp, skillfully chopping trees so that they fell onto precisely predetermined locations. There, the trees could easily be processed into logs by *buckers*.

During the 19th and early 20th centuries, hand saws and axes were the tools used, but they have since given way to the powerful gas-driven chain saw.

Sawyers operated hand- or water-powered saws to make planks and dimensional lumber out of large logs. They had long been among the more highly skilled members of the forest products community, from the development of the saw in about 1500 B.C. In many towns, sawyers were regarded as *millers* because the same waterwheel that powered grindstones was often used to simultaneously run an attached sawmill. Today, however, much of the work that sawyers used to do is done in huge mechanized mills.

Many jobs support or parallel the farmer's role. *Animal scientists*, for example, study the management and production of farm animals, looking for new ways to provide better yields through advances in breeding, handling, feeding, and marketing. *Agronomists* are scientists who work to develop new farming methods yielding higher production and improved quality. *Geneticists* attempt to develop new breeds or hybrids of crops and animals with superior marketable characteristics. They may try to clone (duplicate) outstanding individual specimens in order to widely disseminate and preserve their superior qualities. *Plant pathologists* study plant diseases and look for commercially workable methods of prevention and control. *Agricultural chemists* work largely for the large chemical companies that provide the fertilizers and pesticides widely used in farming.

Animal breeders use specialized knowledge of genetics and herd management to improve breed standards. They operate large artificial insemination programs to perpetuate desirable characteristics and keep careful track of existing animals. Computer analysis is increasingly a major tool used here and in other related occupations.

In recent decades, farming has become big business. With increasing mechanization and ever-larger farms, especially in North America, *agribusinesses* have been formed, which operate farms for the profit of their stockholders or investors. These businesses have been much aided by *agricultural engineers*, who develop labor-saving machines. Although originally designed to help the farmer, some of this machinery has almost made human workers unnecessary. Hundreds of thousands of animals can be kept in huge barns, in which feeding and waste removal are done automatically; often the "farmer" or manager needs only to check the building once a day to see that all is in working order.

Agricultural marketing specialists are essential components of modern agribusiness. By monitoring and surveying the entire production cycle, from producer to

Modern farmers often benefit from studies by trained soil conservationists. (USDA—Soil Conservation Service)

wholesaler to consumer, they develop forecasts of supply and demand for products used by companies such as food processors and agricultural equipment suppliers. *Agricultural economists* analyze conditions that are important to farm production, pricing, financing, and marketing. Many are employed by both government agencies and major agribusiness companies.

Mechanized agribusiness poses a serious threat to the small farmer. Many farmers in North America have gone bankrupt trying to keep up with the most modern machinery and ever-larger farms. Even in the Third World, the Green Revolution has had less impact than was hoped on the small farm, and on the perennial problem of hunger in underdeveloped countries. But the increase in productivity did attract business interests to form larger farms for greater and more profitable production. The future of the independent farmer, on which so much of civilization has depended, is difficult to predict.

For related occupations in this volume, *Harvesters*, see the following:

Beekeepers
Fishers
Hunters

For related occupations in other volumes of the series, see the following:

in *Builders*:
Carpenters

in *Clothiers*:
Fiber Workers
Tailors and Dressmakers
Spinners
Weavers

in *Financiers and Traders*:
    Bankers and Financiers
    Merchants and Shopkeepers
    Stewards and Supervisors

in *Leaders and Lawyers*:
    Political Leaders

in *Manufacturers and Miners*:
    Mechanics and Repairers
    Power and Fuel Merchants

in *Restaurateurs and Innkeepers*:
    Bakers and Millers
    Butchers
    Cooks
    Costermongers and Grocers
    Dairy Operators
    Winemakers

in *Warriors and Adventurers*:
    Soldiers

in *Scientists and Technologists*:
    Biologists
    Chemists

Fishers

The activity of fishing stretches back into the uncharted passages of prehistory. Taken broadly, the occupation includes the harvesting of any of the animal products found in salt water or fresh water. It seems safe to assume that primitive humans took advantage of the protein source provided by fish and other marine life wherever and whenever it was available. A hunting spear could be used to pierce aquatic prey, and a quick hand was often enough to snatch unwary fish from shallow water.

People's constant struggle to find food was not as difficult along shorelines, where a nourishing diet was often available for the easy taking. Fish and shellfish (crabs, lobsters, shrimp, clams, etc.) gathered by hand were major food sources for early shoreline cultures in settings as varied as coastal Siberia, Peru, and North America.

The use of the spear, net, trap, and fishhook as the major tools of the *fisher's* trade are practically universal and of very early origin. Trading between shoreline fishers and inland hunters for food and distinctive local products also had its beginning in prehistoric times and laid the basis for what would become one of the major patterns of world trade. The rise of civilization in the Near East brought the fisher into a broader economic and social context for the first time. Many fishers were able to move beyond subsistence fishing—fishing to provide enough food for survival—to fishing for profit.

In Mesopotamia there were royal fishponds by 2800 B.C. These provided freshwater fish for the tables of many citizens and at the same time produced income for the government. The appearance of large towns and cities created a demand for food that fishing was easily able to satisfy. A sharp distinction was made between the saltwater fisher of the open sea and the freshwater fisher engaged in early *aquaculture*, that is, growing fish and other water creatures for human use. The manager of the royal fishpond was really practicing a form of animal husbandry similar to that of *ranchers* and *herders*. Protecting fish from predators, scattering feed into the water to encourage the growth of hatchlings, stocking the pond, and harvesting the fish population were full-time responsibilities. The fish were harvested with nets and spears, but a cautious balance had to be struck. Fishers had to be careful not to use up all their fish stocks. At the same time, they needed to harvest enough fish to prevent overcrowding. An overcrowded pond could result in fish that were diseased, limited in size, or of poor quality.

State-controlled fishing was the rule in Egypt, having been claimed as a royal right by 3000 B.C. The control of such a major source of food was a matter of major importance to the pharaohs. Large quantities of fish were dried to preserve them. These could be easily stored or distributed as conditions required.

Fishers operating under this strict control became organized as a distinct professional class, with fishing guilds regulating their competition and conduct. The fisher's tackle of hooks, nets, and spears was provided by the government as one of the conditions of employment. Wages were paid as a percentage of the total catch. This system of payment, which rewards high production, was used in fishing cultures around the world in the following centuries, and is still used today.

In China, fish formed an extremely important part of the diet for a large part of the population, and many fishers worked the rivers and coastal areas in small boats to meet the demand. In addition to the ever-present net, spear, and fishhook, many fishing families supported themselves through the use of a very different and highly efficient tool: seabirds called cormorants. The capture and training of cormorants became a very important part of the fisher's trade. Unequalled fishing birds, they could be trained to perch on the fisher's hand and taken out to fishing grounds in small boats. By attaching a string to the bird's ankle and putting a restrictive collar around its neck that prevented it from swallowing its catch, the fisher gained control over an awesome hunter. Tossing the bird overboard and hauling it in after each capture, the fisher quickly amassed a respectable amount of fish. At the end of the day the restrictive collar would be removed and the bird fed and praised for its efforts. This fishing practice eventually found its way to medieval England, but it became a sport of privilege rather than a worker's livelihood. Cormorant fishing is still a part of local coastal economies in China.

Intensive aquaculture was developing in China by 2000 B.C. and quickly established itself as a major branch of the fishing economy. By skimming fertilized fish eggs from the surface of the major rivers and stocking them in convenient bodies of water, freshwater fishers could assure a fairly constant source of fish. The

simple addition of a few yolks from bird eggs to the water near newly introduced fish eggs greatly increased the number of hatchlings that would survive to grow into future food supplies.

Fishers formed a substantial segment of the population of many Mediterranean civilizations during the first thousand years B.C. Fishers operated out of small boats and used weighted nets and fish spears to eke out a subsistence living. By the fifth century B.C., developing patterns of commercial trade gave fishing a major economic importance. The growing seagoing culture of Greece found there was a lucrative market in the long-distance trading of preserved fish. Salted and smoked sardines and herring formed the mainstay of the trade, but other species were widely sold as well. Fishing professionals began to specialize, identifying themselves by the species they caught and the tools they used.

Fishers working on the open water of the ocean or sea constantly worried about how changeable and dangerous the sea could be. Their concern was well-founded. Small, open boats were vulnerable to the onslaughts of freakish momentary squalls as well as major storms. Lost boats and crews are regular calamities—from that day to this—that have threatened every fishing community whose members venture offshore to pursue their livelihood.

The day-to-day life of the offshore fisher has always been one of hard physical labor, directed in patterns that have not changed substantially in thousands of years. In small boats exposed to the full impact of the elements, crews have sailed to fishing grounds that appeared productive. Extremes of temperature, spray, wind, sun, and rain have all conspired to make the fisher's life an uncomfortable one. The constant exposure to cold, wet conditions has always made rheumatism—a painful swelling and stiffening of the joints and muscles—an unhappily common affliction for many fishers. There has always been the probability, too, of less serious injury. Working in a small boat made slippery by water and fish, sailors have been routinely subjected to such inconveniences as broken fingers, cuts, sprains, and bruises.

For every fisher, there were long stretches of time that had to be spent ashore. Seasonal migrations of game fish, dead calms in the ocean, and icy waters are some of the many natural factors that could keep boats beached. Days spent ashore were apt to be busy ones, nonetheless. Nets and other tackle had to be regularly mended; boats made of wood had to be routinely careened (laid on their sides), repaired, and recaulked in a never-ending effort to be prepared for the demands of the sea.

At the fishing grounds, muscle power provided the main hauling apparatus for nets, baited lines, or small traps that were carefully stowed in the bottom of the boat until thrown overboard in a practiced pattern. Depending on the species of fish sought, this equipment might be left in the water, supported by cork or glass floats for hours or days, while the fishers went on to other locations, returning later to pull up their catch. Not until the 19th century did winches and steam engines begin to be used by a few fishers operating from western European and American ports.

Coastal fishers used a variety of nets and traps to catch their prey. (From Picture Book of Graphic Arts)

CROWS ALONG CONEY ISLAND CREEK

Fishers who plied their trade in the sheltered waters of inlets, lakes, and rivers ran somewhat less risk than their offshore counterparts. Their basic tools were similar to those of offshore fishers, however, with adaptations to take advantage of local conditions. A common practice in many cultures throughout the centuries was the construction of fixed fishtraps built of wooden stakes set in a muddy tidal flat. Fish would be trapped there as the tide went out.

Fishing on a small scale might be a solitary endeavor with a lone person setting out traps or baited lines. For most fishers, however, cooperation between several individuals has always been needed. Setting nets, handling boats, and traveling to distant fishing grounds have been group activities. Fishing crews have throughout

Before swimmers took over the beaches, clamming for private or commercial purposes was popular on Coney Island (as was crow-hunting). (By Albert Berghaus, from Harper's Weekly, *March 8, 1884)*

history very often been formed of members linked to each other by ties of family and friendship.

In many cases patterns of group effort in fishing communities remained unchanged throughout thousands of years, particularly in the many areas of the world untouched by the 19th-century Industrial Revolution. In the Bangweulu swamps of Zambia, for example, fishing is an occupation that involves both men and women in a way that would be recognizable to their counterparts of hundreds or even thousands of years earlier. The commercial sale of captured fish is the livelihood of the community and depends solely on human labor. Working without the benefits of motors, winches, or other aids, fishers find cooperative efforts crucial for success. Canoes heavily laden with meal (coarsely ground grain), nets, cooking utensils, firewood, bedding, and building lumber carry the fishers to their camp. A trip lasting weeks or even months will keep the members of the fishing camp apart from their families until the catch is completed, although usually the distance is short enough to permit occasional visits home. The more nets available to be joined together, the larger an area that can be effectively covered. Relatives, friends, and even people from other tribes labor side-by-side, with each person responsible for his own net and entitled to all the fish caught in it. Once the catch has been made, the cooperative effort is over. The drying, transport, and marketing of the haul is the fisher's own chore.

Women fishers in Zambia are no less active than the men, but their catch is not sold, being destined instead for the family table as a major part of the family diet. A cooperative effort is also needed for the type of labor-intensive fishing they engage in. The women form a long line across a section of shallow water and slowly advance together. Each drags a woven, wide-mouthed basket behind her as she wades, and their coordinated movements herd the fish into captivity.

The capture and sale of food fish immediately spring to mind as the objects of the fisher's career, but an enormous trade in other marine products has long directed many fishing boats. In the Mediterranean, the Roman Empire's enormous geographic spread and highly developed trading network created huge demands for a varied assortment of valuable marine captures. Fishers operating dredges from small boats scoured the sea bottom off the north coast of Africa in search of highly prized coral that could be used for jewelry and ornament. The desire to control the richest coral beds and their attendant wealth led to continuing struggles among succeeding Mediterranean powers for dominance, and the fortunes of individual coral fishers depended on their nationality. Here and around the world many fishers became specialized *divers*.

In most cultures fishers formed a tightly knit group of citizens following an occupation that rated neither scorn nor respect from their society. Often related to each other by marriage and joined by a common concern with the practice of their occupation, fishers lived simply and quietly.

The Indian subcontinent was a major exception to this rule. From well over 1000 years B.C., there were many fishers in India working on both coastal waters and inland waters, and their position in society was among the lowest. Only *untouchables* without caste could become involved in the capture and killing of fish, so fishing communities had little interaction with the rest of Indian society. They existed in backwaters and remote districts, living in rigidly segregated villages whose inhabitants had no hope of upward mobility. Entry into the occupation was inevitable for anyone born into an outcaste fishing family, and the trade was practiced with little outside interference or aid.

As the maritime powers of Europe expanded in the 1400s, fishers began to take longer voyages than had ever before been attempted. Indeed, fishers probably preceded by years or perhaps decades explorers such as Christopher Columbus and John Cabot in the discovery of the New World, though the fishing crews generally kept their activities secret from the world. One of the most valuable resources of the Americas was the fish-laden Grand Banks of Newfoundland. Full-rigged ships left European ports in a regular procession on extended fishing voyages to those fertile hunting grounds. Their crews were *sailors* during the voyage, but upon arrival the ship was unrigged, small fishing boats and tackle off-loaded, and a shore-based fishing camp set up for the season.

Before fishing could begin in earnest, the crew had to cut lumber for the construction of the shelters and processing equipment that they would need to preserve their catch. A pier called a *stage* was erected, where the skilled work of cleaning and preparing fish for drying was done. An accomplished *splitter* boned hundreds of fish in an hour's time and passed them on to a *salter*, who covered them with just the right amount of salt for proper curing. Next, the fishers had to dry their catch, putting it on wooden frames called *flakes*, which were then covered with branches. Drying could take as long as three months if there was a shortage of salt. After the fish were fully cured, the crew carefully packed them in waterproof holds in the ship and sealed them for the return voyage home. The crew of these fishing ships worked for shares of the total catch, following the time-honored custom that *whalers* and other fishers had practiced for thousands of years. Skilled crew members were paid more shares than common hands, with the *carpenter* responsible for all the wooden construction being the highest paid member after the captain.

Across the globe, the practices of fishers remained essentially unchanged, passed down within families in shoreline communities from generation to generation. The Industrial Revolution of the 19th century generated some considerable changes in the nature of the equipment and mobility of many fishers, but even for them the day-to-day practices of their occupation remained intact and recognizable. The introduction of steam (later replaced by diesel) trawlers freed fishers from a dependence on uncertain winds and allowed them to range farther and return far more quickly. Power-driven winches and manufactured nets and other accessories lessened some of the routine manual labor involved in the trade. The availability of artificial ice machines made the

Boats and nets are the indispensable tools of most fishers, and require constant care and maintenance. (From Frank Leslie's Popular Monthly Magazine)

time-consuming chore of salting and preserving a catch unnecessary, since fish could be frozen for the return trip to port. Today commercial fishers are able to purchase sonar, depth finders, and other sophisticated pieces of electronic equipment to help ensure their success.

In spite of this technological advancement, the basic facts of hard physical labor, small boats, and unpredictable seas remain. Fishers—men and women—still work long, grueling days when they are out on their boats. Radio sets and vastly improved weather-forecasting networks have greatly reduced the chance of shipwreck and death due to storm, but these are still regular enough occurrences to be a part of every offshore fisher's consciousness.

Huge factory boats, which combine the activities of canneries with floating fishing bases, have appeared in some fisheries. Their crew members, while ostensibly fishers, may in fact have little to do with the actual taking of fish. For some of them, their work may be largely indistinguishable from that of shore-based *factory workers* operating automated machinery in manufacturing plants.

The same technological explosion that has shaped much of the world has destroyed the livelihood of many of the freshwater fishers of developed countries, who had depended on the waters of lakes and rivers for their catch. Industrial pollution has effectively killed the freshwater fishing industry in much of North America and Europe, forcing fishers—whose family roots may stretch back for many generations in the occupation—to seek employment elsewhere.

For related occupations in this volume, *Harvesters*, see the following:

Divers
Farmers
Whalers

For related occupations in other volumes of the series, see the following:

in *Builders*:
  Carpenters

in *Manufacturers and Miners*:
  Factory Workers

in *Warriors and Adventurers*:
  Sailors

Gardeners and Landscape Designers

Gardens were preserves of the rich for thousands of years. This meant that *gardeners* were *servants*, so almost nothing was recorded about them. Large-scale parks have been planned by *landscape designers*, specialists halfway between gardeners and *architects*. In the past 150 years, nurseries have also become common; these are business enterprises where a staff of gardeners raise plants for sale. Before that, gardeners could work only in the gardens of the very few people rich enough to afford them.

The tradition of gardens as special spots of luxury goes far back in time. The story of the Garden of Eden in the Bible is one of the many writings that equate the garden with Paradise. Englishman Francis Condor put it properly when he said:

> When we hear of the introduction of man upon earth, when earth was described as a garden, the occupation of the noblest terrestrial form was to dress it and to keep it.

Luxurious gardens were—and are—found among almost all Mediterranean and Eastern nations. The Hellenistic kingdoms, Rome, and the Islamic countries of medieval times all cultivated them. China seems to have introduced gardens in the Far East, and strongly influenced India and Japan. Though gardens apparently had no part in the cultures of sub-Saharan Africa, the Incas and Aztecs of pre-Columbian America enclosed large tracts as royal pleasure grounds.

From the start, gardening was as much a pastime for the leisure class as a job for workers. Cultivation and use of plants were often enjoyed by the well-educated; a Chinese catalogue of herbs dates from around 2800 B.C. A noble's gardens were also a chance to display taste, and planning them became a major enterprise. A set of plans for an Egyptian garden dates from about 1400 B.C. The structure of the garden shown in the plans is strict enough to imply a set of rules and a long-standing tradition.

Gardens largely vanished from the West with Rome's fall in the fifth century A.D., though monasteries—those havens of culture in medieval Europe—often had gardens of herbs, which were used for medicinal purposes. The pleasure garden did not return for many centuries. In about 1440 a garden book appeared in English for the few who could read. It was called *The Feate of Gardening*, by someone who signed himself Ian Gardener. A century later, cities in northern Italy housed botanic gardens, devoted to raising specimens of rare species. By the 17th century, gardening at last entered a long boom period. Europe's royalty and nobles no longer had to live in fortresses; now, like the Aztecs and Incas, they spent their money on vast pleasure grounds. And, as the Egyptians and many others had done, they designed these for artistic pleasure. Land and plants were reshaped, and the grounds laid out to be seen and appreciated from a designated spot.

As before, working in a garden was a job for servants and also a pleasure for the wealthy. George Washington was a gardener, keeping a careful account of what he was growing, and sometimes working with a spade or shovel, but he left most of the planting and tending to his slave gardeners.

Gardeners who were servants but not slaves could sometimes work their way up to designing parks and gardens, rather than simply tending to them. Lancelot Brown—nicknamed "Capability"—was considered the leader of his field in England. Born in 1716, he graduated from a grammar school and at age 16 went to work on a noble's estate. The other servants on the staff trained him in looking after plants, and after seven years he struck out on his own. Gardening allowed room for a

To create formal arrangements, gardeners planted flowers in strict rows and trained trees to grow in predetermined ways. (From Diderot's Encyclopedia, *late 18th century)*

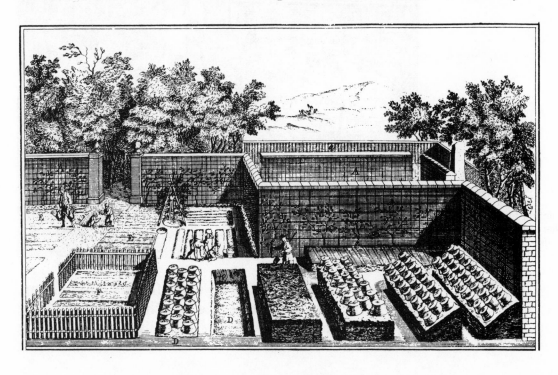

great show of skill, and Brown's skill was outstanding. He was hired by one estate after another, always moving on; at the same time he was moonlighting by selling advice as a consultant. At age 35, he set up a landscaping business in London. Brown became a wealthy man, evidence that there was an excellent market for gardening and landscape design among the rich. But landscaping was also closely related to architecture. The scale, methods, and customers for the two fields were the same, and any gardener who had reached the level of landscaping was likely to drift over into building. This is what Capability Brown did. Likewise, anyone who designed buildings was more likely to landscape than a gardener was.

Nurseries first appeared in the 18th century, and at the start of the 19th were even becoming common. Then, as now, they served people who grew for pleasure as well as the growers of cash crops. They cultivated an extraordinarily broad array of plants. Bernard M'Mahon's *The American Gardener's Calendar* listed 60 kinds of apple trees alone. Boundaries were not clear-cut among the various occupations. The independent owner who managed a nursery might also very well be tending the gardens of one or more customers. The *nursery operator* would even invade the landscaper's territory. Such ambitious operators did not work for a tight circle of the elite, finding instead a larger public in the new middle class. They sometimes placed advertisements in newspapers, like the following from a 1795 *Charleston Gazette*: "The subscriber...purposes superintending ladies and gentlemens gardens in or near the city whether intended for pleasure or profit—he also plans and lays out gardens in the European taste." The subscriber went on to declare his importing and sale of "all kinds of trees, shrubs and seeds, either useful or ornamental..."

With all the new plants, the point of a garden often became more to showcase a variety of flowers than to present a landscape. Parks and gardens came to be looked on as separate things; and the middle class, which had the money for gardens but not the land for parks, made gardening its own. Millionaires continued to hire garden specialists; Andre Parmentier, for instance, worked on Hyde Park, the estate of Franklin D. Roosevelt. But in general, parks became civic projects or money-making schemes. Some such schemes took the form of luxury cemeteries meant to attract paying subscribers. Gardening as practiced by the middle classes employed fewer and fewer people. The nurseries, meanwhile, became massive; America's Ellwanger & Barry cultivated 500 acres. The nurseries and public parks account for almost all the strictly gardening jobs that are left today; the gardener as servant has almost totally disappeared.

Landscape design is now an offshoot of architecture, though less well paid. The designers are expected to have at least a bachelor's degree in landscape architecture, and probably some graduate training as well. There are approximately 15,000 of them in the United States. Some have their own business, and others work for landscaping or architectural firms. Their work now is often a supplement to the architect's; that is, they are expected to arrange a landscape to set off buildings attractively. In addition to parks, they also work on such places as shopping centers and campuses.

People who specifically design gardens now work on a small scale, designing for intimate homes. They mean their gardens to be unobtrusive backgrounds for living. They are a very small class, for most garden owners do their own work and do not want a paid expert interfering.

Nursery operators grow plants, while *landscape gardeners* find most of their work tending the plants once they are grown, trimming and watering them for appearance. Both jobs take skill with the hands, and while with both it is possible to move up from pure manual labor to the more skilled work, a nursery worker is best off starting with a college degree in botanical science.

Nurseries are rural or suburban phenoma; space in cities is far too valuable to be given over to the commercial growing of plants. The floral desires of people who live in cities are generally filled by *florists*, small business owners who arrange and sell fresh-cut flowers or small growing plants. From at least Roman times, florists have provided such services. In modern times, they are linked by telegraphic networks, and a large part of their business comes from supplying flowers for funerals and hospital patients.

In the modern suburbs, gardeners continue to be rare, but their descendants have small businesses in which workers visit homes on a regular schedule—such as once every two weeks during the growing season—to cut the grass and generally tend the grounds. In these areas, where trees are increasingly viewed as valuable assets to a property, *tree surgeons* specialize in pruning and treat-

Floral designers conduct demonstrations and classes for interested amateurs. (Society of American Florists)

ing trees, generally being called in by appointment. Such small businesses also serve larger private institutions. Tree surgeons are likewise employed widely, not least by telephone and electrical service companies, whose wires are at hazard from fast-growing or dying trees. *Groundskeepers* are much in demand for tending to playing fields, such as golf courses; those who care for municipal parks and fields are generally government employees.

For related occupations in this volume, *Harvesters*, see the following:

Farmers

For related occupations in other volumes of the series, see the following:

In *Builders*:
Architects and Contractors

In *Healers*:
Pharmacists
Physicians and Surgeons

in *Helpers and Aides*:
Servants
Undertakers

in *Scientists and Technologists*:
Biologists

Hunters

Hunting is one of the oldest human occupations. Early humans were *hunters* because of the pressing demands of empty stomachs; the pursuit and taking of animals was an essential part of basic survival. Crude spears and clubs were the earliest weapons used by hunters to kill game, and the prey thus gained by direct attack supplemented food that people were able to gather from the surrounding territory.

Continuing observation of prey animals and the success of different hunting methods led to the development of new and superior techniques that paced the continuing evolution of humankind. The appearance of modern humans some 40,000 or so years ago was accompanied by a revolutionary advance in hunting skill. Hunters were well on their way to mastery of the basic hunting knowledge that is still used by subsistence hunters.

Skilled hunters studied the game trails in local hunting grounds and proceeded to construct an ingenious variety of traps that could capture game for them even when they were not physically present at the kill. Pitfalls were dug along trails frequented by large game and armed with sharpened sticks before being cunningly camouflaged. Deadfalls, which crushed their victims when a concealed trigger was stepped on; harpoon and spear traps that transfixed the unwary animals; traps attached to bent trees, which held their catch for the hunter; and leg-hold traps—all were employed in many places around the world.

The technical achievement involved in all these devices marked a major evolutionary step. Hunting, which could be relied on to supply a steady source of protein, enabled families to develop more stable social patterns and allowed each region to support larger populations. The effective use of traps depended on a close and intimate knowledge of the specific area to be hunted, so small nomadic groups that had previously wandered in constant search of food found themselves clustering in semipermanent settlements close to seasonally productive hunting grounds.

Some of the most successful hunting techniques of early humans also demanded close cooperation among several hunters. Picking their spot after careful scouting, a group of hunters after a herd of grazing animals would surround them in a large semicircle and advance, yelling and brandishing their weapons and torches. The terrified animals would flee down the escape route the hunters had carefully left open—and would find that it led to a sheer cliffside, not to shelter. Confronted with the precipice, the prey were unable to stop and fell to their death.

As weapons became more sophisticated and hunters became dependent on the sure flight of thrown javelins and harpoons, or shot arrows, the construction and lucky

Early hunters used handmade tools, among them bows and arrows, to bring down their prey. (From Peoples of the World)

properties of these weapons became a vital concern. Javelins and spears were often painstakingly crafted from mammoth tusks, which had been made pliable by being wrapped in skins and heated in a fire. Hunting skill determined both social status and ability to eat well, so hunters left no avenue unexplored in their desire to constantly improve it. By 20,000 B.C. hunters were participating in ceremonies of magical invocation, which were designed to ensure their success. Cave paintings were thought to have magic powers to attract animals and bring good luck on the hunt. To reinforce this power, the hunters apparently would gather before departing on a hunt and ritually throw their weapons toward the magical figures.

Early hunters also felt a strong spiritual identification with the animals they killed, believing that the qualities of the fallen prey would enter into their own beings. Often an important or feared quarry, like the bear, would be honored by being adopted as the symbol of a clan or hunting society. The weapons, techniques, and religious significance of hunting that developed during prehistoric times have remained among primitive peoples in remote areas across the world until the present day.

Most major changes in the hunter's occupation came as a result of gradual processes. The earliest evidence that hunters used hunting dogs as companions and assistants comes from Cayonyu in Turkey in 9500 B.C. and what is now Lehmi County, Idaho around 9000 B.C. This foreshadowed an association that would become universal and is still current. The domestication of the hunting dog was part of the extremely significant change from a hunting-and-gathering society to an agriculturally based one. Domesticated herds of sheep and goats became common throughout the Near East, and the role of the hunter became that of *protector* of the all-important stock. This new role was at least as important as the former one of primary food provider, since the hunter was now the guardian of a far more secure and appreciated way of life.

The hunter's protective mission took on an added religious significance in Sumer; there predators like the lion were believed to be evil demons, who had to be destroyed. Hunting became a special responsibility of the king, as part of his overall protection of his subjects and their herds. Lions, wild bulls, crocodiles, and asses were the prey of kings and their accompanying hunting parties of *soldiers* and retainers. The technical advancement of weaponry developed for military use was immediately transferred to hunting; and the occupations of hunter and soldier were often inseparably intertwined. Soldiers were hunters for the king, and the pursuit of game was highly valued as a training ground for actual warfare, where human adversaries would be the targets.

Gradually the diligent efforts of the protective hunters secured the settled countryside against predators, and wild game became a relatively minor food source. Then hunting for the first time began to develop as a distinct occupation—not one performed by all. Royal hunts became a form of recreation instead of a necessary duty, and specialized *hunt servants* were employed to make sure that the king's expeditions were successful. *Keepers of the hounds* managed the royal dog pack, while others oversaw the driving of game toward the royal party. Some hunt servants went a step further and specialized in the trapping of live game, which could be released in a chosen location immediately before the arrival of the noble hunting party. This practice led to the establishment of game preserves, where captured animals could be maintained and bred by *gamekeepers*, who were also charged with the maintenance of the preserve's grounds.

After about three thousand years B.C., Egyptian *huntsmen* became a distinct social grouping within their society. They were allowed to follow game on their own, but often acted as attendants for noble parties on hunting trips. The huntsman served as guide, dog handler, and overseer of successfully bagged quarry. He was adept with the noose, net, dart, arrow, and javelin, and on occasion might be called on to train lions for the hunt with the same skill he applied to the royal dog pack. As Egyptian civilization grew in power, the hunting of extremely dangerous game, like hippopotami, was abandoned by the nobility and fell to the professional hunt servant.

Hunting as a sport was still enjoyed by freemen, however, and remained a favorite and valued military pastime.

In ancient China, hunting was originally prized for its food value, but with intensive cultivation and an expanding population, and the resulting agricultural economy, the hunter's role evolved much as it had in the Near East. Hunting became valued as a sport for the emperor and his nobles, and as a training ground for the military. By about one thousand years B.C., most of China's hunting was restricted to massive imperial game preserves, which were presided over by a corps of professional *foresters*, *animal breeders*, and huntsmen responsible for maintaining their stock at peak levels. Hunting was formally included in the jurisdiction of the Ministry of War, and the enormous court hunts periodically held were semi-military exercises conducted by archers selected from the emperor's elite forces. Imperial game preserves staffed by professional gamekeepers would continue in China until the 20th century.

Hunting in ancient India during the first thousand years B.C. was conducted by professionals who used the bow, snares, and spear to capture a wide variety of game. Hunters sold skins and meat to both common town dwellers and royal courts. Kings and nobles maintained game preserves that were used for their pleasure hunting; these gave employment to numbers of gamekeepers and hunters, who specialized in the live capture of wild animals.

The development of the caste system in India and the widespread adoption of Buddhism and related teachings greatly affected the hunter's status. The killing and handling of animals and the consumption of meat came to be regarded as disgusting and ritually impure acts, which could be performed only by *outcastes* or *untouchables*. All hunters fell into this category. As a result they were forced to live in small communities at the fringe of the forest where every villager was a member of the same subcaste. The hunter's status was finalized in 264 B.C. when the great Mauryan king Asoka converted to Buddhism and renounced both hunting as a practice and the presence of meat at the royal table.

In spite of their debased status, professional hunters continued to play a role in Indian society. Elephant hunters sought ivory, which found a ready market, and constructed pitfalls similar to the ones prehistoric humans had used to capture mammoths. Villages of *fowlers* ringed the marshes, and their inhabitants trapped birds in nets and collected eggs for the marketplace. Some used falcons for hunting, while others specialized in the capture and training of ornamental birds, such as parrots and peacocks.

In Europe hunting was a widespread pastime, but few people looked upon it as a separate occupation until the Roman Empire gained dominance. The Roman passion for spectacular combats in the arena created a major business in the capture and sale of live wild animals. Using pits, stockades, nets, and ropes, specially trained hunters made expeditions to the fringes of the empire, penetrating even to central Africa and Asia in their search for ever more exotic specimens for the arena. For special events, military expeditions would sometimes be mounted for the capture and transportation of numbers of elephants, rhinoceri, hippopotami, and the like. Any person who was not a slave had complete freedom to hunt at will for sport or food under Roman law, in accordance with a time-honored European tradition, but this pattern would not endure.

The rise of feudalism in the seventh century A.D. brought with it the rise of royal dominion over European land. The concept that all forest and wasteland was the property of the king and his nobles was a radical departure from previous practice, and it would drastically alter the ability of any person to hunt on his own for either pleasure or profit. In the eighth century, the Emperor Charlemagne instituted a comprehensive forest law system that became the model for subsequent rulers across Europe. Great hunting preserves were established where trespassing of any sort was prohibited. The idea of hunting as an exclusively noble entertainment was introduced, and professional retainers were used to manage the royal hunts. These servants were expert huntsmen who operated within distinct specialties. *Bersarii* were in charge of the hunt of big game; *beverarici* restricted their efforts to the capture of beavers and otters; *veltrarii* were the masters of the king's greyhounds; *falconers* kept hunting birds of prey; and many others oversaw different hunting activities.

Leech-gathering—picking blood-suckers from one's legs and placing them into a keg carried for the purpose—was carried on from ancient to modern times. (Engraving after G. Walker, from Costume of Yorkshire, *1814)*

Hunting gradually became an occupation reserved exclusively for the retainers of kings and nobility in country after country across Europe. Peasants were prohibited from taking deer and other game claimed by the king, and royal huntsmen began to separate into a distinct group of workers. They were set apart from common *servants* by the distinctive green jerkins (vests) they wore and the rapidly evolving specialized vocabulary of the chase.

In the 16th century, hunters organized themselves into guilds similar to those covering other highly specialized workers. In order to become a full huntsman, entitled to wear a hunting sword (later knife) at the belt and a green twig in his hat, a candidate had to complete an apprenticeship that lasted a minimum of three years. During the first year he was known as a *boy huntsman*, or *hound boy*, and was responsible for the care and feeding of the hunting pack, in addition to his general schooling in the huntsman's trade. The second year saw the apprentice progress to the status of *huntsman's lad*, and he was permitted to carry the hunting horn as he assisted on hunts. After three years an examination was given; if the apprentice had managed to amass the specialized knowledge of the trade to his questioner's satisfaction, he became a full-fledged huntsman.

Learning all the information necessary to become a huntsman was not easy. The huntsman had to be totally in command of abundant knowledge about the habits and traits of every animal liable to be hunted in the forest. He also had to be an expert on tracking animals, and to be adept at taking care of hunting weaponry. The intricacies of hunting techniques for all occasions and types of game rounded out the list of basic knowledge. A major specialized vocabulary was needed to deal with this information; huntsmen talking to each other and to their employers spoke in a dialect that was largely unintelligible to the listener not schooled in the subject.

Hunting in medieval and early Renaissance Europe was entirely the prerogative of the nobility and their

By Renaissance times the huntsman was commonly seen as a "nobleman's servant." (By Jost Amman, from The Book of Trades, *late 16th century)*

professional servants. Peasants had to stand aside and suffer any damage to their crops or property inflicted by wild game. As the king's claim to all forest animals became ever more stringently enforced, the unfortunate *poacher* who was caught or even suspected of hunting was subjected to extreme punishment. Eye-gouging, maiming, and execution were rather commonplace penalties.

The hunting of large game, such as boar, deer, and bison, remained totally a privilege of the nobility until the revolutions of the mid-19th century overthrew the absolute rulers of the time and restored hunting privileges to the common citizen. Even by the 17th century, however, some relaxing of the rules against taking small game of various types had occurred. A major trade in the capture, both alive and dead, of small birds for the table developed. *Bird-catchers* used decoys, snares, nets, lures, and guns to kill enormous numbers of feathered prey. Countries that lay along the major migratory flyways developed particularly active bird-hunting industries. In Italy, for example, millions of small birds were still captured yearly through the middle of the present century, and the government made a substantial profit from the sale of licenses to thousands of bird-catchers who used nets or permanently located snares to take birds.

In practice, even though hunting was open to all, the lack of game prevented many persons from attempting to engage in it as an occupation, except for those hunt

By modern times, "the hunt" had become a sport of the rich in many places. (From Diderot's Encyclopedia, *late 18th century)*

servants employed by wealthy gentry continuing to enjoy well-managed blood sports. In England, fox hunting became the most popular 19th-century hunting recreation. Hunting clubs and wealthy individuals kept large packs of dogs and a permanent staff of hunting professionals to manage their sport. *Whippers-in* rode with the pack and made sure that the dogs remained on the trail of the fox and were not diverted by other game. The *earth stopper* worked before the hunt with a pick and shovel, carefully going over the ground and filling in any holes that a fox on the run might attempt to crawl into and halt the chase. The *kennel huntsman* was the dogs' feeder and caretaker.

America's virgin wilderness and bountiful game made hunting an important occupation wherever settlement began to make substantial inroads. Practically every pioneering farmer and homesteader hunted for food, but a small number of people made their livings solely on the strength of their ability to supply growing towns and settlements with fresh meat.

The potentially rich animal harvest of North America's forests attracted early interest from people involved in the lucrative fur trade. In Canada, the earliest French traders bartered for pelts from the Native Americans, but by the late 16th century *trappers* known as *rangers* also penetrated the woods, on their own behalf or as agents of a sponsoring trader. After paying a licensing fee to the government, a trader could go into business and hire half a dozen trappers or so, supplying them with equipment and supplies in exchange for a major portion of their catch. The Hudson's Bay Company, founded in England in 1670, initiated the gathering of furs from the northern territories on a grand scale. Working for this company, hundreds of trappers pushed across most of northern America in pursuit of steadily diminishing beaver and other pelts. The company set up major trading posts, which became like capital cities of the raw land they dominated. The company post outfitted trappers preparing to make their annual fall and winter hunting trips.

The typical 1800 trapper's outfit included the following: a gun, powder, shot, a knife, an axe, 500-600 traps, a barrel of flour, 50 pounds of salt pork, 12 pounds of candles, 30 pounds of drippings, 10 pounds of butter, as well as tea, salt, bacon, blankets, and a tent. The price for this outfit could easily run to five or six hundred dollars. Because this sum was far too great for the ordinary trapper to manage on his own at the beginning of the season, he relied on the credit advanced from the Hudson's Bay Company trading post against his season's haul. This dependency made the trapper sensitive to the rules of company policy. As he left with his pack animals in the fall, he served as an agent of the company's monopoly, and often came into conflict with "free" trappers who were based in the United States and seeking to exploit the same rich territory. The Hudson's Bay Company's legal monopoly in Canada ended in 1859, but its commercial dominance continued; trappers, including Native Americans, continued to depend on its credit system for their outfits. Today, the only major difference in the diminishing trapper's occupation is the use of snowmobiles to transport supplies and check traplines.

The rapid expansion of the American population and a strong demand for skins of all sorts gave rise to another specialized hunting professional. The *buffalo hunter* was an expert at mass slaughter and used high-powered rifles to massacre staggering numbers of bison for their skins and choice portions of meat. The buffalo hunter's path was easily traceable by the mountains of rotting carcasses littering the landscape and by the sharp decline of the once-massive buffalo herds. The hunt itself was an easy chore. After settling himself into a comfortable location, the hunter shot the herd leader—and then methodically killed as many of the remaining animals as he desired, since they would stand stolidly by their fallen leader.

As early as the 1820s huge parties of 600 to 1,000 wagons would transport hunting expeditions to the kill, and by 1860 more than 650,000 buffalo had been killed by commercial hunters. In the middle part of the 19th century the introduction of the repeating rifle greatly increased the number of buffalo that could be killed. The expansion of railroads across the American West created a ready market for meat to feed their construction crews and also provided a ready means for the shipment of massive numbers of skins to Eastern markets. Using a repeating rifle, a buffalo hunter could easily kill upwards of a hundred buffalo in a few hours; as a result the annual take escalated tremendously. Between 1872-1874, for instance, professional buffalo hunters destroyed nearly 5,500,000 animals. This bloodthirsty pace managed to almost totally destroy the entire buffalo population by the turn of the century, and buffalo hunters became anachronisms as the result of their too zealous harvest.

Most major changes in the hunter's occupation came as a result of gradual processes. With the widespread destruction of game habitats in the 20th century, hunting generally became an occupation practiced by a very limited number of people outside of private hunting preserves. Primitive subsistence hunters existed in ever-diminishing numbers in remote areas of the world.

Hunters in the far north, such as the Eskimo, long continued their enduring system of hunting, which depended on dog sleds and kayaks. But hunting patterns there were finally changed by the introduction of modern technology in the mid-20th century. Access to power boats, high-powered repeating rifles, and snowmobiles dramatically altered the life-style of the Eskimo hunter. Traditional techniques, which had placed a high value on the skilled making of weapons and the management of extended solo hunting trips, were no longer valued. Mass-produced hunting weapons and rapid transport quickly debased the skilled hunter's high social position and made his occupation a mere job. Similar cultural derangements have occurred throughout the world where traditional subsistence hunters have had their lives abruptly transformed by the availability of modern machinery.

Even once impenetrable jungles were pierced by modern economies and technology, as the exploitation of natural resources increased. In Africa, *big game hunters*—many fewer now than earlier in the 20th century—work as guides for wealthy sportsmen and women seeking trophy heads. Other wilderness regions also support a small number of professional *hunter/guides*. A very few individuals work as hunters catching live specimens for zoos. An even smaller number work as *trappers*, hired to preserve large stands of timber from destruction by beavers. But other career opportunities for hunters are practically nonexistent.

In recent years a growing awareness of the fragility of the remaining game populations has placed many of the surviving animals under the protection of strictly enforced game laws. However, a steady demand for items such as ivory and rhinoceros horn attracts significant numbers of people to the illegal and hazardous work of poaching. Surreptitious hunters using poisoned darts and wire snares stalk protected game under the cover of darkness and wage armed warfare with the *rangers* and *game control officers* patrolling the preserves.

Hunting seems destined to employ fewer people as wilderness areas shrink and conservation efforts within them increase. The survival of sport hunting will undoubtedly continue to offer employment to a select group of professionals who work as guides and game managers.

For related occupations in this volume, *Harvesters*, see the following:

Farmers

For related occupations in other volumes of the series, see the following:

in *Clothiers*:
Hatters

in *Helpers and Aides*:
    Servants

in *Leaders and Lawyers*:
    Inspectors
    Police Officers
    Political Leaders

in *Manufacturers and Miners*:
    Weapon-Makers

in *Scholars and Priests*:
    Priests

in *Scientists and Technologists*:
    Biologists

in *Warriors and Adventurers*:
    Soldiers

Whalers

To early humans, the stranding of a whale ashore was seen as a gift from the gods and a once-in-a-lifetime opportunity to feast and revel in a seemingly inexhaustible mountain of food. The active pursuit of whales by people armed with weapons who were intent on killing and using the products of the carcass was begun by the Vikings, probably after 500 A.D. Fearless sailors, the Vikings practiced shore whaling as a sideline to their main occupations of plunder and fishing.

When a whale was sighted from shore, the call went swiftly through the seaside village. Small crews quickly launched heavy rowing boats and followed in hot pursuit of the passing whale until they had closed within a few yards of the creature. Standing in the bow of the boat, a powerful and skilled crew member known as the *harpooner* hurled his weapon deep into the whale's body, trying to hit a vital area. The boats' crews pursued the wounded animal, striking it with additional harpoons until it was killed. The pursuit was a perilous one, as an enraged whale could easily splinter a wooden boat and kill its occupants with a blow from its enormous body or tail. The killed whale was taken in tow by the whaleboats, brought back to the village, and hauled up on the shore. The blubber was cut off in long strips and rendered in large kettles to release its oil. The pattern of shore whaling developed by the Vikings would remain virtually unchanged until the 19th century and would be used by whalers of many different nations.

In the 12th century A.D. Basque sailors became the first professional whalers, making the capture of whales the central goal of their working lives. Like the Vikings, they were restricted in their hunting to the waters immediately off their coastline. Norman sailors chased whales off the Bay of Biscay until the 15th century, when the number of whales close offshore had declined to the point that it was no longer possible to make a living hunting them.

In spite of the dwindling numbers of easy-to-hunt coastal whales, the valuable commodity of whale oil spurred a growing industry. By the late 16th century, whalers from England, Holland, France, Denmark, and Germany were outfitting ships equipped for extended voyages to the North Atlantic fisheries, where hunting was still excellent. During the end of the 17th century, Holland was the dominant whaling nation, supporting over 260 ships and 14,000 whalers in the trade. As England became the dominant sea power in the 18th century, it used the whale fisheries as a training ground for the *sailors* who supported its economy and military might. By the 19th century, however, American whalers had attained total dominance of the trade.

The succession of different nationalities to the whaling leadership reflected directly on the strength of their maritime establishments. Whalers were first and foremost sailors. The typical whaling ship of the 19th century carried a crew of 40 to 50 members, all of whom had common seamen's duties in addition to their whaling tasks. They sailed in slow, heavily timbered ships built to withstand the ice commonly found in the northern waters of the major fisheries. The crew of a whaler worked on shares, an arrangement that had become traditional over the centuries. Each crew member was paid a fixed wage and a percentage of the ship's total catch. Each member's share was negotiated at the time of signing on and reflected the value placed on his special skills. A master harpooner, for example, was a highly prized and crucial factor in a ship's successful voyage and could be expected to receive a markedly higher share than a common seaman.

The actual techniques of whaling and the daily lives of the men engaged in it changed very little over the centuries. In the whaling grounds, a *lookout* was always posted at the masthead and constantly scanned the horizon for the quarry. When the cry of "There she blows!" alerted the crew that a whale had been spotted, the deck became the scene of feverish activity. Each boat crew hustled into its boat, was lowered into the sea, and raced to be the first to the whale. As soon as the first boat arrived, the harpooner directed the crew until he was satisfied that he had reached the exact spot where his cast of the harpoon would do the most damage. When the harpoon had embedded itself in the whale, the boat's crew made haste to let out the carefully coiled line attached to it as the wounded whale sounded and dove deep beneath the surface. A carelessly placed foot or hand snagged by the furiously uncoiling line could mean instant amputation or death by drowning. While the whale was out of sight beneath the surface, the boat's crew endured a suspenseful vigil, for there was always the chance that the animal would surface directly beneath them and capsize or smash the whaleboat. If all went according to plan, the whale's reappearance would be the signal for the boats to come together and strike it with additional harpoons until the wounded, exhausted animal floated on the ocean surface. The whalers would then finish it off with lances and take the carcass in tow back to the waiting ship for processing.

The operation of stripping the carcass of its oil-rich blubber and usable bone was called *flensing*, and was an extremely unpleasant, stinking task. Crew member with iron spikes attached to their boots swarmed over the carcass wielding blubber spades. Great 20-to-30-foot strips of the whale's skin would be cut from the carcass and hoisted to the ship's deck. The *baleen*, the flexible bone widely used for corset stays and other purposes in the 19th century, was also taken. Three or four hours of hard work stripped the whale of all its usable parts, and then it was cut loose from the ship's side and allowed to sink.

While some crew members plied their blubber spades, others were charged with processing the raw blubber into liquid oil. As the huge blubber strips swung onboard, they were cut into small pieces and loaded into huge cast-iron kettles in a procedure called *trying out* or *making off*. The blubber was cooked until it liquefied and then was strained into casks, which would be stored in the ship's holds. This rendering operation was a dirty job that produced great clouds of grease-laden smoke, which coated everything on deck with a sticky layer.

Once their prey was spotted, whalers took to their boats and sped after it. (From Century Illustrated Monthly Magazine)

Whalers of the northern fisheries usually sailed forth in the spring and autumn for seasonal voyages. The whale operation began to decline in the North Atlantic by the mid-19th century because so many were being killed. Some whaling ships took to spending the winter in the Arctic, so that they could be assured of maximum competitive advantage when the spring thaw came. The enormous pressure placed on the Atlantic whale fisheries by ships sailing from New England and New York took its toll, and whalers began to make greatly extended voyages beyond the shipping lanes in search of prey. A sailor signing on to a mid-19th century whaler never knew how long it would take his ship to return to port. The whaler would stay out until its holds were full, and commonly made voyages lasting a year or more and that could lead to the North and South Pacific.

The Industrial Revolution brought about the first substantial changes in an occupation that had remained

Along with whalers, other sea hunters roamed the Atlantic and Pacific; this sealing crew in the Falklands is wielding bats against young seals. (Authors' archives)

basically unchanged for a thousand years. By 1860, the harpooner standing anxiously in the bow of the pursuing whaleboat was replaced by a *gunner* sighting a small swivel cannon armed with a harpoon. The harpoon itself was the subject of ingenious experiment aimed at speeding up the kill and reducing the crew's exposure to danger. Hollow harpoons or rifle bullets loaded with prussic acid or strychnine quickly killed the prey. By 1865 the explosive harpoon gun was perfected and in widespread use, while fast steam-powered ships shortened the time a whaler had to be at sea.

Even as these technical advancements were put into common use, however, the devastating depopulation of the worldwide whale fisheries was making hunting increasingly unprofitable. The petroleum industry's rise in the United States sealed the whaling industry's fate. Because of the decline in the demand for whale oil, most whalers were forced to forsake their trade, and they migrated en masse to other ships, working as *merchant seamen*.

Whaling became a very small and specialized trade practiced by a handful of nations. Japan and the U.S.S.R. became the predominant sponsors of the new hunt and brought increasing technical ability to the problem of profitably bringing whales to harvest. Modern whalers have replaced the lookout posted at the masthead with a technician poring over a sonar screen. A typical hunting vessel is a massive, sophisticated factory ship with a crew of 400, which launches high-speed motorized whaleboats armed with sophisticated cannon-fired explosive shells. The crew members in charge of the processing of the captured whales tend an automated disassembly line, which takes the entire whale aboard through a ramp in the bow of the ship and ejects a cleaned carcass at the stern. There has been an increasingly vocal international outcry against the continued depletion of the diminishing whale population and fewer people are engaged in the occupation every year, possibly signaling the end of this long-plied trade.

For related occupations in this volume, *Harvesters*, see the following:

Fishers

For related occupations in other volumes of the series, see the following:

in *Warriors and Adventurers* (forthcoming):
Sailors

Suggestions for Further Reading

For further information about the occupations in this family, you may wish to consult the books below.

General

Auboyer, Jeannine. *Daily Life in Ancient India, 200 B.C.-700 A.D.* New York: Macmillan, 1968. Includes excellent background information and detail about farming and hunting on the Indian subcontinent and its role in society.

Montet, Pierre. *Everyday Life in Ancient Egypt in the Days of Ramses the Great.* London: Edward Arnold, 1962. Useful setting of farming and hunting in the greater context of dynastic Egyptian society.

Farmers

Bloch, Marc Leopold Benjamin. *French Rural History.* Berkeley and Los Angeles: University of California Press, 1966. An extremely detailed study including information on tools and social status; especially strong for medieval and earlier periods.

Blum, Jerome. *Lord and Peasant in Russia: From the 9th to 19th century.* Princeton: Princeton University Press, 1961. Details the status of Russian serfdom, exploring the chains binding peasant farmers to the land.

Critchfield, Richard. *The Golden Bowl Be Broken.* Bloomington: Indiana University Press, 1973. On peasant life in four Third World cultures, with an emphasis on the Green Revolution and its impact on traditional farmers.

Duby, Georges. *Rural Economy and Country Life in the Medieval West.* Columbia, S.C.: University of South Carolina Press, 1968. Full of information about the everyday life and social status of peasant farmers in Europe.

Hartley, Dorothy. *Lost Country Life.* New York: Pantheon, 1979. Especially good for English medieval history of the life-style of common people.

Hsu, Cho-Yun. *Han Agriculture: The Formation of Early Chinese Agrarian Economy.* Seattle: University of Washington Press, 1980. Very informative, not only on crops and techniques, but also on the social status of farmers and their place in the national economy.

Huggett, Frank E. *A Day in the Life of a Victorian Farmworker.* London: George Allen & Unwin, 1972. An informative snapshot, with supporting history, of the English 19th-century farm laborers and their life-styles.

King, Franklin H. *Farmers of 40 Centuries; or Permanent Agriculture in China, Korea, and Japan.* New York: Harcourt & Brace, 1927. Offers good descriptions of traditional farming practices before widespread introduction of 20th-century techniques.

Nair, Kusum. *The Lonely Furrow: Farming in the U.S., Japan, and India.* Ann Arbor, Mich.: University of Michigan Press, 1969. Provides cross-cultural contrasts; especially useful for modern Japan and U.S. migrant workers.

Schlebacker, John T. *Whereby We Thrive: a History of American Farming 1607-1972.* Ames, Iowa: Iowa University Press, 1972. Very substantial and useful, especially when tracing the American farmer's love of mechanical improvements.

Smith-Halsey, Richard. *A Tour of Four Great Rivers in 1769.* Port Washington, N.Y.: Ira J. Freidman, 1969. A revealing and well-written travelogue of the state of agricultural America in 1769.

Streuves, Stuart, ed. *Prehistoric Agriculture.* Garden City, N.Y.: Natural History Press, 1971. Scholarly but readable, with reams of information about its subject, worldwide.

Zeuner, F.E. *A History of Domesticated Animals.* London: Hutchinson, 1963. A basic work on the subject, tremendously informative and useful for any consideration of the topic.

Gardeners

Hyams, Edward. *A History of Gardens and Gardening.* London: J.M. Dent, 1971. A useful review.

Hunters

Coon, Carleton S. *The Hunting Peoples*. Boston: Little, Brown, 1971. Good treatment of modern primitive hunting peoples around the world—from Eskimos to Bushmen.

Hobson, Erich. *Fair Game*. New York: Arco, 1980. Very comprehensive historical survey, including both weapons and techniques and social importance.

Whalers

Scammon, Charles Melville. *The Marine Mammals of the Northwestern Coast of North America, described and illustrated, together with an account of the American whale-fishery*. New York: Dover, 1968; reprint of 1874 edition. A complete, contemporary survey of whaling during its heyday in the late 19th century.

Stackpole, Edward A. *The Sea-Hunters: The New England Whalemen during Two Centuries, 1635-1835*. Westport, Conn.: Greenwood Press, 1972. Full of useful information about the earlier whaling industry.

INDEX